EXECUTIVE COMPENSATION AND SHAREHOLDER VALUE: THEORY AND EVIDENCE

EXECUTIVE COMPENSATION AND SHAREHOLDER VALUE:
Theory and Evidence

Edited by

JENNIFER CARPENTER

and

DAVID YERMACK

Stern School of Business
New York University

NEW YORK UNIVERSITY
NYU STERN
LEONARD N. STERN SCHOOL OF BUSINESS

KLUWER ACADEMIC PUBLISHERS
DORDRECHT / BOSTON / LONDON

Library of Congress Cataloging-in-Publication Data is available.

ISBN 0-7923-8179-3

Published by Kluwer Academic Publishers,
P.O. Box 17, 3300 AA Dordrecht, The Netherlands.

Sold and distributed in North, Central and South America
by Kluwer Academic Publishers,
PO Box 358, Accord Station, Hingham, MA 02018-0358, U.S.A.

In all other countries, sold and distributed
by Kluwer Academic Publishers, Distribution Center,
P.O. Box 322, 3300 AH Dordrecht, The Netherlands

Printed on acid-free paper

Printed and bound in Great Britain by MPG Books Limited, Bodmin, Cornwall.

Table of contents

JENNIFER CARPENTER AND DAVID YERMACK
New York University

Introduction: executive compensation and shareholder value

Executive compensation has gained widespread public attention in recent years. The pay of top American executives has reached unprecedented heights compared with the past, with top executives in other countries, or with the wages and salaries of typical employees. This level of managerial compensation, with annual remuneration of $10 million or more for many executives, has spawned a great deal of publicity in the media and has attracted the attention of the US Congress, the Securities and Exchange Commission, the Financial Accounting Standards Board, and the Internal Revenue Service, as well as criticisms from shareholder activists, labour leaders, and political candidates.

The extraordinary levels of executive compensation have been achieved at a time when US public companies have realized substantial gains in stock market value. Many have cited this coincidence as evidence that US executive compensation works well, rewarding managers who make difficult decisions that lead to higher shareholder value. Others have argued that executives have received overly generous streams of wealth that sometimes bear little relation to company performance and should rightly belong to shareholders, citing such statistics as the diversion of more than 10% of the typical large company's equity to stock options and other compensation plans. Many have also criticized the compensation process as rife with conflicts of interest between executives, directors and consultants.

This volume presents research papers from a conference on these issues sponsored by the Salomon Center of New York University's Stern School of Business. In the Salomon Center tradition, the conference included leading-edge academic research as well as discussion and debate among scholars, informed practitioners and public officials concerned with issues related to executive compensation.

Part I of this volume contains papers investigating the association between executive compensation and gains in shareholder wealth, with perspectives on both American and international companies. Many critics of executive pay contend that the important link between compensation and performance is minute or even non-existent.

J. Carpenter and D. Yermack (eds.), Executive Compensation and Shareholder Value, vii–ix.

Steven Kaplan's paper, 'Top Executive Incentives in Germany, Japan and the USA: A Comparison', summarizes his research into the structure of managerial incentives in three leading industrial economies. The paper shows that both compensation and the threat of dismissal are significantly related to company stock price performance in all three countries, with the magnitudes of these effects appearing quite similar. However, when stock and option ownership are considered, US executives appear to have stronger performance incentives than their German and Japanese counterparts.

Using evidence from ten different European countries, Martin J. Conyon and Joachim Schwalbach offer an illuminating look at the diversity of managerial incentives in that continent. The authors show that despite the freer flows of labour and capital implied by the integration of Europe's economies, large disparities exist in how executives are paid in different countries. Neither company size nor governance structures are able to account fully for these differences.

Brian Hall's paper, 'A Better Way to Pay CEOs', contains a detailed investigation of the compensation of American CEOs. Hall discusses the growing use of stock options in US compensation arrangements and documents that the overwhelming majority of performance incentives received by CEOs come from options and direct stock ownership. He argues that the growing use of options has resulted in substantial improvements in the intensity of managerial incentives over the last two decades, to the point where a typical CEO stands to gain annual rewards approaching $10 million for moving his firm from poor performance to excellent performance. He concludes by arguing for improvements in the ways that companies award stock options and keep track of their value.

Part II of this volume explores the process by which executive pay is established in American companies. Kevin Hallock's paper, 'Dual Agency: Corporate Boards with Reciprocally Interlocking Relationships', investigates the pervasiveness and consequences of a well-known source of conflicts of interest in the process for setting managerial pay. Hallock's results indicate that approximately 20% of all large firms have board of directors members who sit on one another's boards. Further evidence suggests that CEOs of these companies receive higher compensation, and that other agency problems may also be more likely to occur.

Executive stock options, the fastest-growing element of executive compensation, are the topic of Part III of this volume. Steven Huddart's paper, 'Patterns of Stock Option Exercises in the United States', offers a thorough introduction to the structure, valuation, and taxation of employee stock options. Huddart discusses why employees' decisions about when to exercise their options have important consequences both for option valuation and incentive properties. He presents empirical results showing that most employees exercise options well in advance of their expiration. These surprisingly strong patterns are partly but not completely explained by tax considerations and employee risk aversion.

Brian Main shows how differently stock options have been treated by UK companies compared with their US counterparts. Main documents a growing use of stock options in the UK beginning in 1984, followed by a reintrenchment about a decade later. This change, which appears to have been motivated by a political backlash against executives' gains from stock options, represents an interesting contrast to the American experience which involved an unrestrained increase in the use of options over the same period. Main shows that accounting-based performance bonuses have supplanted stock-based rewards as a source of UK managers' incentives, a pattern that he labels unfortunate.

The papers in this volume should be of interest to corporate executives with responsibility for establishing executive compensation practices, as well as compensation consultants, financial analysts, accountants, money managers, and public officials.

PART ONE

STEVEN N. KAPLAN
University of Chicago

1. Top executive incentives in Germany, Japan and the USA: a comparison*

INTRODUCTION

Executive compensation and corporate governance systems have received an increasing amount of attention, from academics, government, the popular press and businesses themselves. Much of this attention has focused on differences between the US system and those of its strongest industrial competitors, Germany and Japan. The US corporate governance system is generally characterized as a market-based system. US capital markets are liquid and company ownership is relatively unconcentrated. Managers are supposedly monitored by an external market for corporate control and by boards of directors usually dominated by outsiders. The German and Japanese governance systems, in contrast, are characterized as relationship-oriented systems. Ownership in Germany and Japan is concentrated and capital markets are relatively illiquid. Managers there are allegedly monitored by a combination of banks, large corporate shareholders, and other intercorporate relationships that are maintained over long periods. An external market for corporate control is small, if not absent. Table 1 summarizes these differences.[1]

The differences in governance systems, in turn, are usually associated with differences in managerial behavior and firm objectives. One view argues that the close financial ties and relationships in Germany and Japan reduce agency costs and allow investors to monitor managers more effectively than in the USA.[2] According to this view, there are lower costs to changing poorly performing management because banks and large shareholders have the power to make needed changes. Costly hostile takeovers or proxy fights are avoided.

This view has also been associated with claims that German and Japanese

* This paper was prepared for the Conference on Executive Compensation and Shareholder Value at New York University on October 24, 1997.

[1] See also La Porta *et al.* (1996) and Shleifer and Vishny (1997) for a discussion of international differences in corporate governance.

[2] Grundfest (1990), p. 98. See also Aoki *et al.* (1994), Hoshi *et al.* (1990, 1991), Lipton and Rosenblum (1991), Porter (1992), Prowse (1990).

J. Carpenter and D. Yermack (eds.), Executive Compensation and Shareholder Value, 3–12.

Table 1. Comparison of German, Japanese, and American corporate governance systems

	Germany	*Japan*	*USA*
Executive compensation	Moderate	Low	High
Board of directors	Management/supervisory	Primarily insiders	Primarily outsiders
Ownership	Concentrated: high family/ corporate/bank	Less concentrated: high bank/high corporate	Diffuse: non-corporate/ non-bank
Capital markets	Relatively illiquid	Somewhat liquid	Very liquid
Takeover/control market	Minor	Minor	Major
Banking system	Universal banking	Main banking system	

firms are less concerned with or affected by short-term earnings, and, therefore, better able than US firms to manage for the long-term (i.e. invest in projects with long-term payoffs). This position assumes that current stock prices can diverge from long-term shareholder values. Because banks and large shareholders have both better information and more power to use that information than the widely dispersed shareholders of the typical US company, financing is more readily available for value-increasing long-term projects in Germany and Japan. The supposed monitoring and information advantages have led some to call for the US corporate governance system to imitate aspects of the German and Japanese systems.[3] Others, however, argue the alternative view that the German and Japanese systems entrench managers and employees at the expense of shareholders. Banks, allied with incumbent managers, may receive abnormally high fees or interest rates in exchange for agreeing to bail out managers (and their companies) in cases of poor performance and financial distress even if it is not efficient to do so.[4]

As suggested above, many observers have been quick to distinguish the US system from its German and Japanese counterparts, and to draw conclusions about the nature of those differences. Most of these distinctions were initially based on anecdotes, cases, and surveys. In contrast, my work (Kaplan, 1994a,b; Kaplan and Minton, 1994) provided some of the first systematic evidence on how the German and Japanese systems operate and how they differ from the US system. The results challenged those anecdotes.

3 In particular, see Porter (1992) who argues that the US system leads to underinvestment.

4 See Abegglen and Stalk (1985), Baums (1992, 1993), and Coffee (1991) for a discussion of these views. Milgrom and Roberts (1992) and Roe (1993) are also sympathetic to this conclusion.

In this chapter, I summarize and discuss the implications of the results in those three papers. Executive turnover in all three countries increases significantly with poor stock performance and earnings losses. Executive compensation in Japan and the USA is also related to stock returns and earnings losses. The effects in all three countries are generally economically and statistically similar. The fortunes of German and Japanese top executives, therefore, like those in the USA, are strongly affected by stock performance and current cash flows. Sales growth, a measure of market share, plays a smaller role. There is no evidence, therefore, that US managers have any more incentive to be short-term oriented than their German and Japanese counterparts. There appears to be, however, one substantial difference between the USA and the rest of the world – stock and option ownership. US managers own more stock and options. I conclude the paper with an explanation for my results and with some conjectures on the relative advantages and disadvantages of the three governance systems.

What incentives do corporate governance systems provide?

As noted above, most discussions of managerial motivations in Germany, Japan, and the USA are based on anecdotes or surveys. I decided to test the anecdotes by asking one simple question: What incentives do the different corporate governance systems really provide to top managers? Specifically, by understanding why top managers are fired and why they are paid more, one can infer what incentives they actually have.

The relation of managerial rewards and punishments to firm performance

Kaplan (1994a,b) studied corporate governance in the largest companies in the three countries (42 in Germany, 119 in Japan, and 146 in the USA) from 1980 to 1988. These analyses focus on the top group of managers or operating executives in each firm in these countries. These executives are management board members in Germany; representative directors in Japan; and executive directors in the USA.

In Germany, the management board (the Vorstand) comprises the seven or eight top managers and includes the Chairman who is the equivalent of the CEO. German firms also have a supervisory board (the Aufsichtsrat) which is the equivalent of an outside board in the USA. Under the German co-determination system, the supervisory board includes both shareholder and labour representatives. In larger public companies, the supervisory board will typically have 19 members.

In Japan, the typical board has 21 members, almost all of whom are insiders. The president is the chief executive officer or CEO. In each company, three or four directors, including the president, are given special rights to represent the company. These are known as the representative directors.

Finally, in the USA, the firm is governed by a board of directors of typically

13 or 14 members. Approximately one-third are insiders and two-thirds are outsiders. The CEO is the most powerful of the managers and directors. The executive directors are the operating managers who also are on the board of directors. This group typically includes four or five members and always includes the CEO.

The first question I asked is what kind of performance causes the top operating managers in these firms to lose their jobs? In technical terms, this involved estimating the following regression:

$$\text{Probability of losing job} = \alpha + \beta \times \text{Performance} + \epsilon$$

I used four measures of firm performance: company stock returns; sales growth; change in pre-tax income as a fraction of total assets; and a dummy variable which is equal to 1 if pre-tax income is negative. Sales growth is meant to be a measure of market share, and is presumably, a measure of long-term management. The dummy variable for negative pre-tax income, in contrast, which indicates that accounting earnings are less than operating and financial expenses, is perhaps the most short-term measure of performance.

The turnover results are presented in Figures 1–3. In all three countries, managers are more likely to lose their jobs when their company's stock performs poorly (Figure 1). In all three countries, managers are more likely to lose their jobs when their company experiences an earnings loss (Figure 2): Japanese and German managers are approximately twice as likely to lose their jobs in a year with a loss than in a year with positive earnings. Interestingly, the sensitivities or relationships in the three countries are not different from one another in a statistical sense. Finally, managers are more likely to lose their jobs in Japan and the USA when sales growth is poor (Figure 3). Surprisingly, German managers are unaffected by poor sales performance. Furthermore, sales growth is less important in Japan than earnings and stock performance.

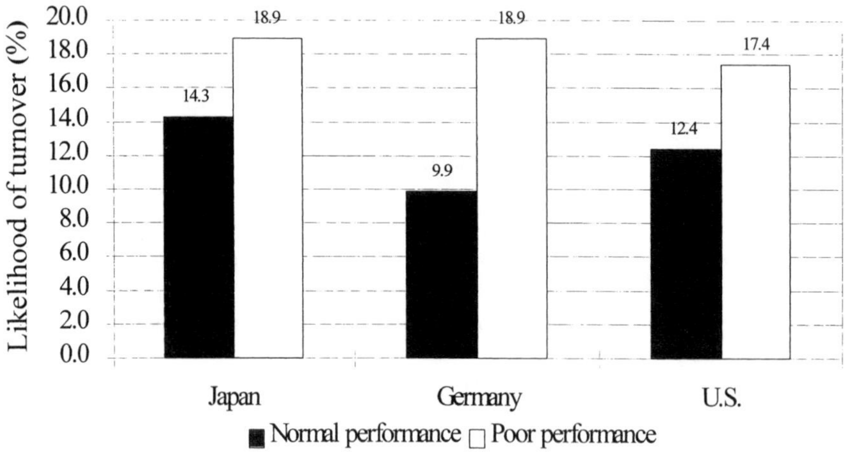

Figure 1. Top executive turnover and stock returns.

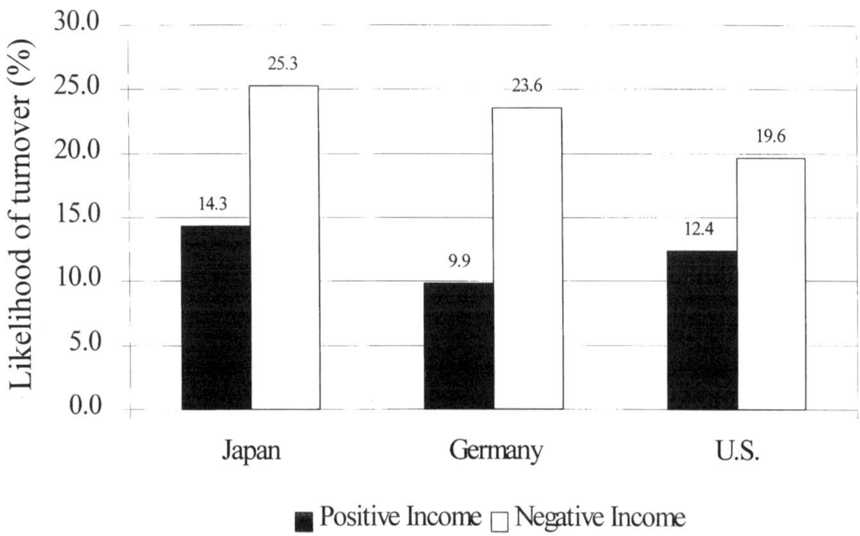

Figure 2. Top executive turnover and negative income.

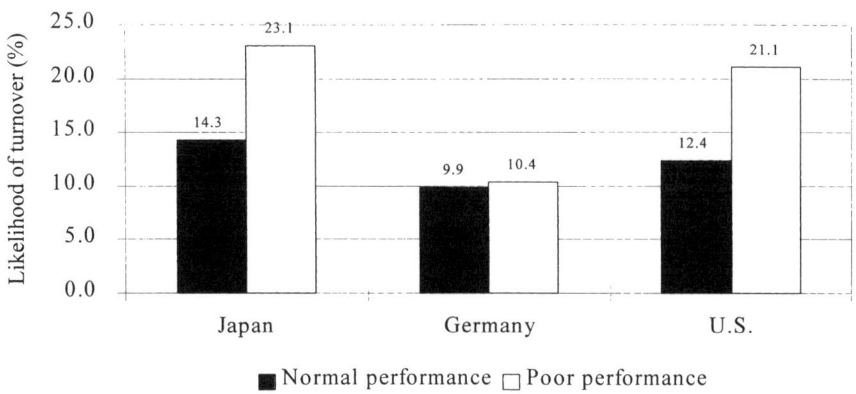

Figure 3. Top executive turnover and sales growth.

The second set of tests considers top management compensation and its relationship to firm performance in Japan and the USA.[5] It is true, as is commonly believed, that Japanese executives earn lower levels of cash compensation than US executives. The important question for incentives, however, is when are the top managers in those two countries paid more? To answer this, as with turnover, I estimated a simple regression using the same four measures of performance:

---

[5] These data were unavailable for German executives.

$$\text{Percentage change in compensation} = \alpha + \beta \times \text{Performance} + \epsilon$$

The results are presented in Figures 4 and 5. As is the case with top executive turnover, Japanese management compensation is strongly related to earnings, stock, and sales performance, and again the sensitivities in Japan and the US are virtually identical. A two standard deviation change in stock returns leads to roughly an 8% increase in compensation in both Japan and the USA. An earnings loss leads to a 13% pay cut in Japan and a (statistically indistinguishable) pay cut of 18% in the USA.

What do these results for turnover and compensation mean? Three very different systems generate very similar outcomes. The fortunes of German and Japanese managers (and US managers) are tied to stock performance and current cash flows – measures that some would refer to as short-term. Furthermore, the punishments and rewards for German and Japanese managers are not more sensitive to sales growth – a measure some would refer to as long-term – than those of the USA: if anything, they are less sensitive. It is difficult, therefore, to reconcile these findings with the view that German and Japanese managers are more patient, i.e. they can ignore current cash flows to pursue increases in market share or sales growth. Finally, it is also difficult to reconcile these results with the view that the US system is more short-term.

These results, in turn, suggest two broader conclusions. First, successful corporate governance systems respond to current measures of performance, earnings and stock prices. Second, the current stock price reflects a firm's current and future health.

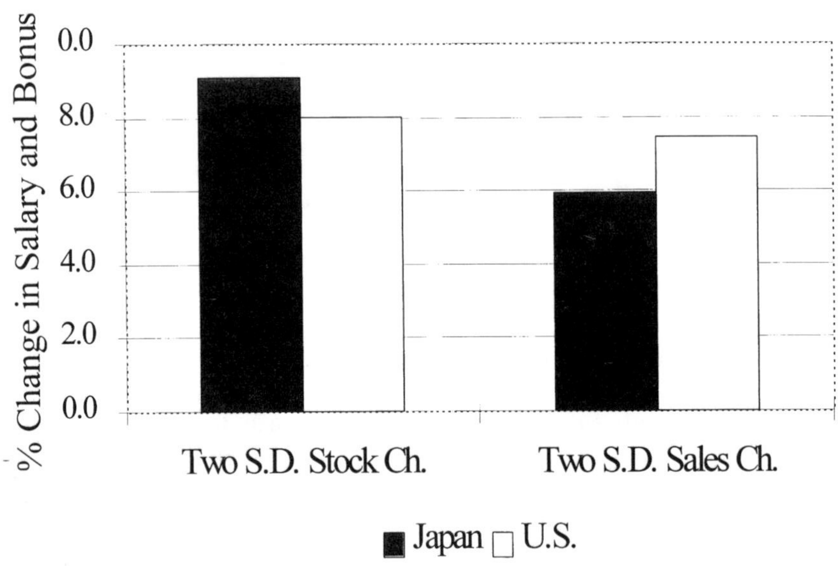

Figure 4. Top executive compensation and performance.

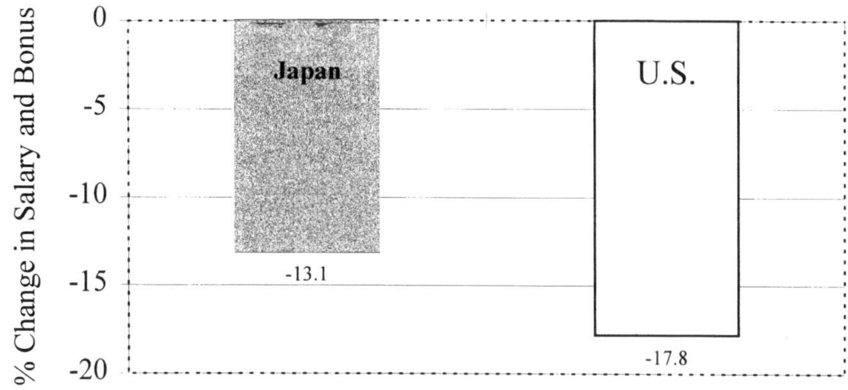

Figure 5. Top executive compensation and earnings loss.

The impact of banks, corporate shareholders, and relationships

The results for top executive punishments and rewards relative to stock and earnings performance in Germany and Japan cannot be driven by an external market for corporate control because no such market exists in either country. This section considers possible explanations for or sources of the turnover performance and compensation performance results. As noted earlier, the most likely forces behind those results are banks, large corporate shareholders and other intercorporate relationships. Kaplan (1994a) and Kaplan and Minton (1994) present evidence on the importance of those forces in Germany and Japan, respectively.

The first question the two papers ask is when do banks or large shareholders take an active interest in the sample companies? The papers measure such an interest as particular types of board appointments. In Germany, I studied new appointments to the supervisory board. In Japan, we studied appointments of 'outsiders' to the board, where outsiders are individuals who are not lifetime firm employees but have previous work experience at a bank or large shareholder. Both supervisory board appointments in Germany and outside appointments in Japan are increasingly likely as stock performance deteriorates. These results are consistent with the governance relationships in Germany and Japan playing a monitoring and disciplinary role.

Kaplan and Minton (1994) continue with a more detailed comparison of outside appointments in Japan. Appointments of bank directors in Japan (outsiders affiliated with banks) increase with earnings losses, as well as with poor stock performance. Appointments of outsiders in Japan also increase with measures of the intensity of the relationships: appointments of bank directors increase with a firm's borrowings from banks; appointments of corporate directors increase with shareholder concentration and with corporate group affiliation.

While these results are consistent with the governance relationships in Germany and Japan playing a monitoring and disciplinary role, they are also consistent with an insurance interpretation in which the presence of an outsider signals to suppliers, customers or others that the bank or the affiliated corporation will support (i.e. bail out and, therefore, insure) the appointing firm. Kaplan and Minton (1994) distinguished between the two interpretations by considering the relationship between outside director appointments and top executive turnover. Turnover increases substantially in periods when outsiders are appointed, even when controlling for firm performance. We interpret this result as saying that banks and corporate shareholders do play a monitoring and disciplinary role in Japan. In this sense, the relationships appear to at least partially substitute for the more market-oriented US control mechanisms.

Why are the results so similar?

The bottom line of my three papers is that very different corporate governance systems in Germany, Japan, and the USA generate similar outcomes. The key similarity is that all three countries have successful market economies. In this section, I discuss why I think the results tend to be similar.

To understand this, it helps to look at two dimensions (see Table 2). First, governance differences should be less important when firms cannot survive if they fail to maximize. That will be true when product markets are competitive, government subsidies are small and few (economic) rents are lying around. In those circumstances, managers face two basic choices: maximize or fail. Managers who do not maximize, and often their firms, will not survive.

Second, governance differences become less important as firms require more capital. When industries are growing or changing and firms need capital, it is difficult to obtain financing to pursue excessive or unprofitable growth. In other words, if a firm's corporate governance structure allows its managers to waste resources, that firm will not be able to obtain financing. Given that competitive product markets and competitive capital markets dominate most capitalist economies, the similarity in the German, Japanese, and US results should not be particularly surprising. Governance, in a real sense, takes care of itself when industries are growing and changing, and when industries are competitive.

Table 2. When do governance differences matter?

	Competitive markets	*Uncompetitive markets*
Growing/changing	Least	Somewhat
Mature	Somewhat	Most

Governance differences will matter most in mature industries or in non-competitive industries where firms can survive for substantial periods without maximizing and waste substantial resources in the process. Jensen (1986) described such firms and industries as being susceptible to large agency costs of free cash flow. Oil companies in the USA in the 1980s and many Japanese firms in the late 1980s fit this description.

WHICH SYSTEM PROVIDES THE BEST INCENTIVES?

The final and most interesting question to be addressed is which governance system, if any, provides the best incentives?

On the dimensions I studied in my research, the three systems are similar. There is no clear difference between the three governance systems in responding to poor stock and earnings performance. That result has been confirmed by the recent responses of German companies to competitive difficulties and exchange rate movements. Japanese companies also have responded in 'American' ways to its recession and strong yen. There also do not appear to be clear differences in incentives to manage for the short-term or for the long-term.

As I argued in the previous section, there are good reasons to believe that the similarities are the product of successful market economies. In other words, as long as an economy is competitive or market-based, governance systems will be pushed by the market to become relatively efficient. Different systems, then, will generate satisfactory outcomes.

While the three systems are similar in many respects, the US system has important advantages over the other systems. In particular, the US system provides better incentives to firms that are already performing well. Such firms will include those in mature industries or in industries that are not perfectly competitive. The better incentives come from the fact that US managers hold much larger stock and option positions than managers in Japan (see Figure 6) and, probably, managers in Germany. Because they own more shares, it is arguably less tempting for US managers to overinvest or waste the extra cash that a successful firm generates.

Since the period studied in my papers, the differences between the US and other systems almost certainly have increased because of the wealth of the USA. CEOs has become increasingly sensitive to the performance of their companies' stock. This increased sensitivity has been driven by a substantial increase in the use of equity- and option-based compensation in US firms. In a recent paper, Hall and Liebman (1997) found that from 1980 to 1994, the average annual CEO option grant (valued at issuance) increased more than seven-fold from $145 thousand to just under $1.2 million. As a result, by 1994, equity-based compensation made up almost 50% of total CEO compensation, compared to less than 20% in 1980.

If the US corporate governance and incentive system is superior, one might expect that other countries would start to copy the USA. This appears to be happening. In Japan, it is no longer illegal to issue executive stock options (their issuance, however, is still constrained by regulations relative to those in the USA). In Europe, according to accounts in the popular press, the use of stock options for executives and boards is increasing. I would expect the movement to US incentives to continue.

REFERENCES

Abegglen, J. and G. Stalk (1985). *Kaisha, the Japanese Corporation*. New York: Basic Books.

Aoki, M. (1990). Towards an economic model of the Japanese firm. *Journal of Economic Literature*, **28**, 1–27.

Aoki, M., H. Patrick and P. Sheard (1994). The Japanese main bank system: An introductory verview. In Aoki, M. and H. Patrick (eds.), *The Japanese Main Bank System: Its Relevancy for Developing and Transforming Economies*. Oxford: Oxford University Press.

Baums, T. (1992). Corporate governance in Germany: The role of the banks. *American Journal of Comparative Law*, **40**, 503–526.

Baums, T. (1993). *The German Banking System and its Impacts on Corporate Finance and Governance*. Working paper, Institut fur Handels- und Wirtschaftsrecht, Osnabruck, Germany.

Coffee, J. (1991). Liquidity versus control: the institutional investor as corporate monitor. *Columbia Law Review*, **6**, 1277–1368.

Hall, B. and J. Liebman (1997). *Are CEOs Really Paid Like Bureaucrats*? Working paper, Harvard University.

Hoshi, T., A. Kashyap and D. Scharfstein (1990). The role of banks in reducing the costs of financial distress in Japan. *Journal of Financial Economics*, **27**, 67–88.

Hoshi, T., A. Kashyap and D. Scharfstein (1991). Corporate structure liquidity and investment: evidence from Japanese panel data. *Quarterly Journal of Economics*, **106**, 33–60.

Kaplan, S.N. (1994a). Top executives, turnover, and firm performance in Germany. *Journal of Law, Economics, & Organization*, **10**, 142–159.

Kaplan, S.N (1994b). Top executive rewards and firm performance: a comparison of Japan and the US. *Journal of Political Economy*.

Kaplan, S.N. and B. Minton (1994). Appointments of outsiders to Japanese boards: determinants and implications for managers. *Journal of Financial Economics*.

Kaplan, S.N. (1997). The evolution of US corporate governance: we are all Henry Kravis now. *Journal of Private Equity*.

Kester, W.C. (1991). *Japanese Takeovers: The Global Contest for Corporate Control*. Boston: Harvard Business School Press.

La Porta, R., F. Lopez-de-Silanes, A. Shleifer and R. Vishny (1996). *Law and Finance*. NBER working paper 5661.

Lipton, M. and S. Rosenblum (1991). A new system of corporate governance: The quinquiennial election of directors. *University of Chicago Law Review*, **58**, 187–253.

Milgrom, P. and J. Roberts (1992). *Economics, Organizations and Management*. New Jersey: Prentice Hall.

Porter, M. (1992). Capital disadvantage: America's failing capital investment system. *Harvard Business Review*, 65–83.

Prowse, S. Institutional investment patterns and corporate financial behavior in the US and Japan. *Journal of Financial Economics*, **27**, 43–66.

Roe, M. Some differences in corporate structure in Germany, Japan, and the United States. *Yale Law Journal*, **102**.

Shleifer, A. and R. Vishny (1997). A survey of corporate governance. *Journal of Finance*, **LII**, 737–784.

MARTIN J. CONYON AND JOACHIM SCHWALBACH
University of Warwick, UK and Humboldt University Berlin

2. Corporate governance, executive pay and performance in Europe

INTRODUCTION

Executive pay and corporate governance issues continue to attract wide academic, media and policy attention.[1] The very high salaries enjoyed by senior executives in corporations in some economies are often contrasted with the relatively low pay received by executives in other economies. The case of the USA (high CEO pay) and Japan (low CEO pay) is an obvious example. At the same time, the stark differences in the corporate governance structures between such economies is often highlighted. For instance, the governance system in the USA and UK (which stress the market for corporate control as a means of correcting managerial failure) is compared with the German and Japanese system (which stress long-term commitment). There is an implicit assumption that these alternative systems of corporate control and governance may result in quite different economic outcomes and in particular patterns of executive pay.

Despite the continued fascination with executive pay issues, as well as what constitutes an optimal corporate governance mechanism, there has been very little academic research comparing executive pay across economies. Furthermore, little has been attempted by way of seeing how these international patterns of executive pay vary according to the boardroom governance structure that particular economies have adopted. In part this can be attributed to the difficulties in obtaining and assembling the requisite data. The primary aim of this paper, then, is to present some new evidence on the pattern of European executive pay in the mid-1990s. Specifically, we address the following questions:

1. Are differences in European executive pay correlated with job level/function? Are the returns to job level the same through-out the managerial hierarchy?

---

[1] For instance, Jensen and Murphy (1990) and Murphy (1998) document the effects of corporate performance and scale on executive compensation. A review of recent UK research is found in Conyon *et al.* (1995). Mayer (1996) outlines recent evidence underlying economic performance and corporate governance.

J. Carpenter and D. Yermack (eds.), Executive Compensation and Shareholder Value, 13–33.

2. Are differences in European executive pay correlated with corporate scale? Are the effects of company size the same at different levels of company size?

3. Are differences in European executive pay correlated with country specific effects? If country characteristics are important in shaping executive compensation, are these effects similar for each country?

4. Are differences in European executive pay determined by differences in corporate governance regimes? Do economies with radically different board structures have different levels and structures of executive pay?

Each of the above, we argue, are consistent with alternative explanations of executive pay determination. Executive job level and company size are important proxies for managerial talent and should clearly influence executive pay outcomes. Cross-country variation in pay can provide evidence of the degree to which managerial labour markets are internationally integrated. Finally, the system of corporate governance (particularly board structure) may give rise to different patterns of executive pay. This may occur because different board structures are associated with different arrangements for establishing executive pay. We hope to cast some light on each of these issues.

More generally, an analysis of the level and structure of European executive pay is warranted given the lack of existing evidence. We use pay data derived from expert remuneration consultants presented at the macro level for each of ten European economies separately. Despite the difficulties in using macro data (specifically in attributing causation) we believe our analysis to be useful. We can compare directly, using international data, the level and structure of executive compensation across a range of European economies. Accordingly, we can describe how executive pay levels and structure vary according to job function, corporate size, international integration, and basic board governance structures.

Corporate governance and executive pay

Corporate governance

Corporate governance refers to the way in which firms are directed and controlled. Shareholders are the ultimate owners of the firm who typically delegate decision making authority to a management team. The fundamental question arises: are the interests of the management team aligned with those of the ultimate owners? If there are incentives for the interests of each group to diverge, then we have to examine those forces that provide potential realignment. This is the domain of corporate governance. European economies have evolved different mechanisms to resolve these agency issues. In this section we wish to describe the main features of the European governance scene by focusing on two economies: Germany and the UK.[2] To fix ideas we will follow Nickell (1995) who usefully characterizes two governance types. Type I is characterized by large, well-developed equity markets where the equity in each company is controlled by shareholders. These are institutions or private investors who are not closely involved with the firm. In type I economies hostile take-overs (mergers and acquisitions) are (relatively) easy. The market for corporate control disciplines the management team. In type II, equity markets are organized so that a substantial amount of equity in each company is controlled by shareholders. These shareholders have a long-term commitment to the company. Hostile take-overs do not occur (friendly take-overs may). The market for corporate control (hostile take-over) does not function.

Economies such as the UK and USA are examples of type I governance systems, whereas Japan and Germany conform to type II systems. Type I and type II economies can use different internal and external governance mechanisms (or some mixture) to align the interests of managers and owners. These may promote long-term value maximizing activity. Type I economies make extensive use of the threat of take-over, and the actual take-over mechanism, to persuade management to pursue profit maximization (external control). Type I economies have outside or non-executive directors who sit on the company board who act as representatives of shareholders and monitor the performance of the management team (internal control). Type II economies are characterized by dual boards where banks have an important role in representing the owners interests (external control).

British corporate governance

The British corporate governance system shares many of the features of the US arrangements. The company board is made up of executive and non-executive directors corresponding to US inside and outside directors. The average size of a British board is about 11 members. The non-executive proportion of the board is usually between 0.5 and 0.6. During the 1990s corporate governance and compensation issues resulted in a number of policy documents, and stock exchange listing requirements, which changed the British corporate governance scene. The Cadbury (1992), Greenbury (1995) and latterly the Hampel (1998) Committees all argued for increased disclosure of directors' emoluments and adherence to 'best practice' governance arrangements.

Evidence on recent developments in British corporate governance is given in Conyon and Peck (1998). The fraction of the board made up of outside directors has been increasing. Also, companies have been adopting key board committees. All listed companies now have audit committees. Most large stock market companies (95%) have remuneration committees. The majority of these compensation committees are made up of outside directors only. Furthermore, large companies are inclined to separate the posts of CEO and chairman (85%).

---

[2] A more complete review is provided in Charkham (1995).

German corporate governance
The system of corporate governance in Germany is significantly different from the anglo-American system. By law, large corporations have a two-tier board structure consisting of a supervisory board (Aufsichtsrat) and a management board (Vorstand). The management board is the center of corporate decision-making and is responsible for strategy formulation and implementation into day-to-day business. Typically, the management board consists of more than two full-time employed executives who are appointed by the supervisory board for a period of up to 5 years, whereby re-appointment is possible. The management board reports at least once a year (usually three or four times a year) to the supervisory board about the current state and intended business policy of the corporation.

The supervisory board has the responsibility to monitor the activities of the management board. It is composed of at least three members depending on the size of the corporation. According to the Co-determination Act of 1976, half the members are made up of elected employees' representatives and the other half is elected by shareholders. Shareholders usually assemble once a year (Hauptversammlung) mainly to judge the work of the management board and supervisory board.

The German system of corporate governance in large corporations is known for its close ties to financial institutions, dual shareholdings and interlocking directorates. The representatives of the shareholders in the supervisory board are in many cases drawn from the executive ranks of other large corporations or financial institutions where some of them have major stakes in the corporation. In general, executives of banks and insurance companies are involved in many supervisory boards. By law, a single executive cannot be on more than ten boards simultaneously, which does not apply to institutions he or she represents. For instance, the chairman of the largest bank in Germany, the Deutsche Bank AG, is a member of the supervisory board of large corporations like Bayer, Daimler-Benz (chairman), KHD (chairman), Linde, Lufthansa, Mannesmann, Münchner Rück, RWE and Veba. Among the largest 100 companies, about 10% of the shareholders' representatives on the supervisory board are from financial institutions in 1992.[3] Banks are also represented in the shareholders assembly even if they do not keep stocks of that company. By law, banks have so called proxy voting rights (Depotstimmrecht) if shareholders ask the custodian bank to represent them in the annual assembly. In some cases, this could add up to about 80% of the votes held by banks in the shareholders' assembly (Baums, 1994).

Another feature of the German system of corporate governance is the dual shareholdings in the sense that company A holds stocks of company B and vice versa. Companies A and B could consist of many sub-companies which is called circular shareholdings. Both types can be found in Germany. Figure 1

[3] See "Stellungnahme des Bundesverbandes deutscher Banken". In: *Zeitschrift für Bankrecht und Bankwirtschaft*. 1994, 6(1), 77.

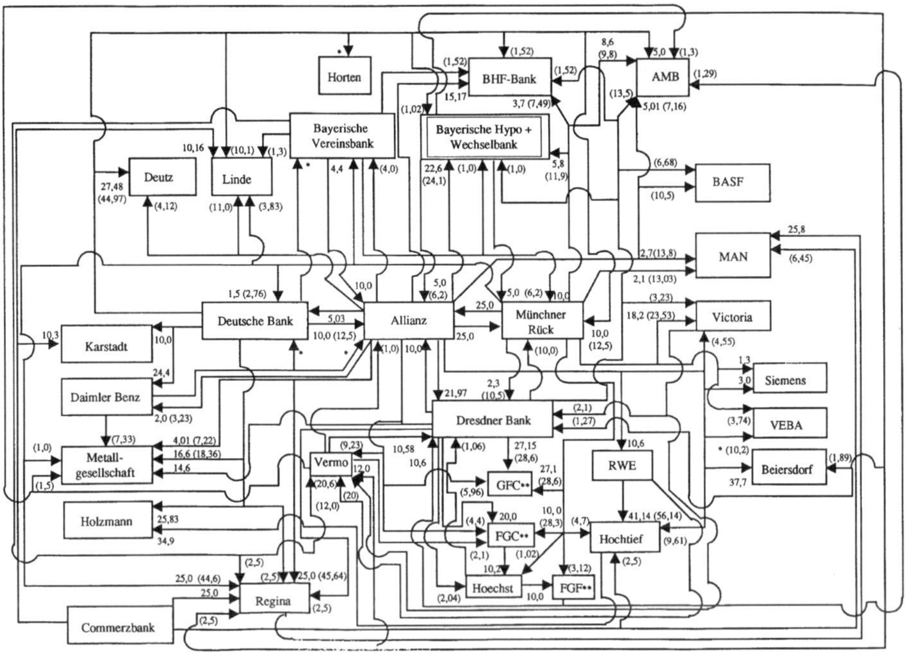

Figure 1. The German corporate governance structure. Note: numbers without brackets show direct stake holdings, numbers in brackets show direct and indirect stake holdings. *less than 5%; **GFC, Gesellschaft für Chemiewerte mbH, FGC, Frankfurter Gesellschaft für Chemiewerte mbH, FGF, Frankfurter Gesellschaft Für Finanzwerte

provides an example for a network of dual and circular shareholdings in 1996/97, illustrating how major financial institutions (Deutsche Bank, Dresdner Bank, Commerzbank, Bayerische Hypo- und Wechselbank, Bayerische Vereinsbank, BHF-Bank, Münchner Rück, Allianz, AMB and Victoria) held (direct and indirect) shares among themselves and to non-financial companies.

Bank representatives in corporate supervisory boards, proxy voting rights and dual/circular shareholdings may result in interlocking directorates. Various studies have shown that among the 100 largest companies there are personal links to at least two other companies of the same size group (Biehler and Liepman, 1988, Pfannschmidt, 1995). In addition, there is evidence that interlocking directorates became increasingly a strategic issue in the sense that banks, for instance, see the personal links as way of obtaining an information advantage which may improve their position as creditors.

European corporate governance

In our empirical work below we are interested in examining how the level and structure of European pay is correlated with differences in corporate governance systems and board structure. Boards may influence executive pay outcomes by directly setting executive pay and by monitoring executive effort. However, the incentives for outside (non-executive) directors in type I governance systems to effectively monitor and evaluate directors may be blunted (see Nickell, 1995; Hart, 1995; Jensen, 1993). This may be due to lack of information on the part of outside directors, lack of private rewards to the monitoring function, or indeed capture by the incumbent CEO who may have appointed them in the first place or control information flows to them. These problems may not be so acute in type II systems which effectively divorces the management from monitoring function. In our empirical work, then, we simply allow for international differences in executive pay outcomes according to type I and II systems.

On a practical level one has to identify the European type I and II economies in terms of their board structure. Such an exercise may be influenced by judgement. We have identified the type I and II board structures according to the Korn Ferry (1996) method. Accordingly, the following five economies, from our European pay data set of 10 economies, were classified as type II economies with two-tier board structures: Germany, Austria, Denmark, the Netherlands, and Switzerland. Those economies which were classified as type I (single board economies) are the UK, Ireland, Italy, Spain and Belgium.[4]

Executive compensation

Both type I and type II economies are characterized by asymmetrical information between owners (or their representatives) and the management team. Agency models predict that incentive contracts of various kinds (relating pay to observed measures of performance) will be observed in such situations. The owners of the firm have incomplete information about the performance (or effort) of the management team. They are concerned with maximizing the long-term prospects (value) of the enterprise. This is an increasing function of the effort expended by management, but is also affected by random shocks (which may be aggregate, firm or industry specific). Both effort and the shock are not observable *ex ante* (the performance function is non-separable in its arguments) but performance is observable (or may be approximated) *ex post*. It is usual to suppose that management is both risk and effort averse and holds an outside job opportunity. The optimal (linear) contract will tie some proportion of management pay to observed profit. Consider two contracts. Under contract 1 the firm pays the manager a fixed wage and receives the residual income. Here the incentive for effort is minimal as pay is not related to outcomes. Under contract 2 the firm receives a fixed income (dividend) and the manager receives the residual income (profit). Incentive to management effort is very large (and so is risk and compensation). The second-best (share-cropping) contract is the intermediate case where some income depends on performance (see Nickell, 1995).

---

4 Korn-Ferry classify Belgium as a mixed system country.

Much of the academic research on executive pay focuses on US data. The high pay received by executives at US leading companies is sometimes contrasted with the salaries received by directors in Japanese companies and elsewhere (see Kaplan, 1994, Crystal, 1992). In comparison to the voluminous US literature, there are relatively few European studies. Of those that do exist most are single country studies and do not explicitly compare executive pay across Europe.[5] The two variables that characterise these type of regression analyses are corporate performance and company size. Empirically, the most important predictor of executive pay is company size reflecting the returns to managerial talent in large companies (see Rosen, 1992). Company performance variables (either market or accounts based) appear to play less of a role in shaping executive pay (see Conyon *et al.*, 1995).

In our empirical study we have available two measures that may proxy managerial talent. First, is job position. We are able to identify executive pay for one of five job levels ranging from CEO to middle manager. Economic theory (e.g. tournament models)[6] would suggest that the pay is positively related to job level. Second, we can identify the pay of an executive in one of six size class bands and, in common with micro-econometric work on the determination of pay, we can examine the returns to company scale. We provide such for a range of European economies in 1996.

European differences in executive compensation

Assembling data on executive pay across European countries is difficult (see Abowd and Bognanno, 1993). Different country governance structures (type I and II), legal and accounting systems and alternative ways of measuring executive compensation complicates the data assembly exercise. Usually, there are no unifying datasets which allow cross-country comparisons.

However, in this chapter we use as our primary data source information on executive compensation by the European Independents Remuneration Network (EI-RN) supplied by P-E International to provide evidence on the cross-national level and growth in European pay. The data refer to the period 1996. There are 10 countries included in the review (Austria, Belgium, Denmark, Germany, Ireland, Italy, Netherlands, Spain, Switzerland and the UK). The data collection methodology involves survey data assembled by important compensation consulting companies throughout Europe. In total 2,846 companies are represented across the 10 economies, accounting for 30,288 incumbents.[7] The EI-RN survey represents one of the largest and most extensive reports of its kind in Europe. Because of the way in which executive pay is defined in this data set

---

5 For instance, some recent European studies of executive pay determination include: Conyon (1997), Cosh and Hughes (1997), Main *et al.* (1996) – UK. Grasshoff and Schwalbach (1997) – Germany. Angel and Fumas (1997) – Spain. Eriksson (1996) and Eriksson and Lausten (1996) – Denmark. Alcouffe (1998) – France.

6 See Lazear and Rosen (1981), Lazear (1989, 1995).

7 The distribution of companies across Europe is given in the appendix.

(i.e. it is essentially total cash compensation; see below) we supplemented this pay data source with data from a Towers Perrin survey. This allowed us to construct a richer pay variable which includes, for instance, the value of long-term incentive plans (see below). Our analysis also seeks to explain whether there are systematic differences in executive pay according to types of board structure. In particular, we wished to identify those European economies which have so called two tier board structures (see above).

Before formally stating the hypotheses, we describe in more detail our primary data source. The Remuneration in Europe data (P-E International) contains information on total cash compensation and bonus for executives in each country. The pay information can be collected for job levels and corporate size. We defined our first pay measure (PAY1) as total cash/remuneration, which is defined as base salary + variable cash.[8] Base salary means the annual contractual salary (P-E International, 1997, page 6). Variable cash includes bonuses (performance and/or merit), commissions, profit-share or other non-guaranteed payments (P-E International, 1997, page 7). Total cash/remuneration excludes the estimated value of stock options and other equity held by directors (this may be more appropriate for some economies than others – see Abowd and Bognanno, 1993 and our supplement data below). The data for each of the countries is transformed to a common unit using the currency conversion rates supplied by Remuneration in Europe. The descriptive data below are reported in D marks, sterling and Ecus.

There are five job levels. Job level 1 is defined as the most senior full time executive of the company.[9] Job level 2 is usually a director of the company.[10] Job level 3 is the head of a major department who is not a director. This person may be referred to as a senior manager.[11] Job level 4 is a senior manager responsible for establishing new methods of implementing a defined strategy and plans within a given discipline. Finally, Job level 5 is a middle manager of the company concerned (typically reporting to levels 3/4).

Our data set also contains pay information by employee size bands (of which there are a maximum of six).[12] Band 1, 1–99 employees; band 2, 100–249 employees; band 3, 250–499 employees; band 4, 500–999 employees; band 5, 1,000–4,999 employees; and band 6, 5000 or more employees. Each country provides data in 4–6 size bands depending on the most appropriate end-point to produce valid data (P-E International, 1997, page 6).

---

[8] PAY2 and PAY3 use data from Towers Perrin and are described below.

[9] The individual is responsible for defining strategy, in agreement with the stated policy of the board and/or shareholders. He/she can make suggestions to the board regarding the adoption of policy. He/she is responsible for the profit/loss of the organization and the company's overall management; he/she reports to the board shareholders.

[10] The individual will usually sit on the board or at least the executive committee of the organization. He/she is reponsible for developing strategy and planning within the business unit function. He/she reports to job level 1.

[11] The individual is responsible for planning and implementation of strategy within a department and usually reports to levels 2.

[12] Employees are defined as the number of full-time equivalent employees at the company.

Conceptually, then, our estimated pay equations which follow can contain 300 data points (i.e. $5 \times 6 \times 10$); however, in practice the actual number is less. Some countries have fewer size band data (e.g. Austria) and in some of the regressions reported below we can only focus on CEOs (rather than the full compliment of executives). This latter issue arises when we are matching CEO only data from Towers Perrin.

The supplementary Towers Perrin data set contains a much richer specification of the pay variable which we are keen to exploit. The data are available for CEOs in 1995 only. In addition, three of our economies were excluded due to lack of data (Austria, Denmark, and Ireland). We defined our second pay measure (PAY2) as total cash compensation plus compulsory and voluntary contributions, perquisites and the value of long-term incentives. Compulsory contributions include employer contributions and expenses for social security, compulsory benefits and termination indemnities. Voluntary contributions are employer contributions for private retirement, life insurance programmes, and medical and other employee benefit plans. Perquisites include the annual cash value of cars, club memberships and other sundry perquisites. Finally, the value of long-term incentives is usually the value of executive stock options. The value of PAY2 was arrived at in local currency and deflated by the exchange rate given by EI-RN.

The final pay measure (PAY3) tries to make an allowance for differentials in European personal rates of income taxation by examining the after-tax value of pay. This measure aims to focus more on the purchasing power of income, rather than the pre-tax cost to the employer. To this end we calculated PAY3 simply as (1–tax rate) $\times$ PAY2. The tax rates that we use are drawn from Abowd and Bognanno (1993) and are presented in Appendix Table A2.

Using the information contained in our main data set we can model executive pay as:

$$y_{ijk} = w + \alpha_i + \beta_j + \delta_k + \epsilon_{ijk} \tag{1}$$

where y is the log of pay in job level i in company size band j in country k. The pay measures we used are PAY1 to PAY3. The term α_i is the contribution of the job level in explaining the cross-section variation in y, β_j are the contribution of corporate scale to the variation on y and δ_k is the contribution of country specific effects (see below). ϵ_{ijk} and w are the equation error and an arbitrary constant. Since α_i, β_j and δ_k are indicator variables, identification requires that one variable be excluded in estimation. We chose the lowest size class band and job level. Arbitrarily, we chose Austria as the excluded country. All other dummy variables are relative to these.

Equation 1 is not amenable to structural or causal interpretation (see Schmalensee, 1985). However, as a reduced form model we can test some important statistical restrictions. We tested that job level or position has no effect on the level of pay ($\alpha_i = 0$), and whether the effects of job level are identical ($\alpha_i = \ldots = \alpha_4$). We would expect CEOs to earn more than middle managers. Similarly, we can test the importance of company size in the pay regression (i.e. $\beta_j = 0$). The null hypothesis is that pay outcomes are not related to the size of the company. Furthermore, we can test whether the size effect is the same within each employee band. $\beta_2 = \ldots = \beta_6$ (where 6 is large company and 2 is a small company).

Finally, we introduced a role for country specific effects. Increased European integration and the effects of factor price equalization would tend to predict that executive compensation should be equal for individuals with similar abilities and characteristics. If this process was complete, then after controlling for individual factors the country specific effects should be negligible: $\delta_k = 0$ implies that pay outcomes are independent of country-specific factors. If valid, this suggests that pay outcomes depend not on country factors but instead purely on other factors (e.g. human capital, job position, company effects). However, if country effects are important we can test whether executive pay responds the same way in all countries by testing the restriction that values of δ_k are identical, that is, there are no differences in the country effect on executive pay.

We are also interested in the impact of board structure on executive pay. Having classified the European economies into governance types I and II we define an indicator variable (board) which equals 1 if the economy is type II and 0 otherwise. Since board and the industry dummies are linearly dependent identification requires the exclusion of the country effects. Accordingly, we estimate:

$$y_{ijk} = w + \alpha_1 + \beta_j + \lambda \text{Board}_k + \epsilon_{ijk} \tag{2}$$

where λ is the (cross section) proportional effect of a type II board system on the level of executive pay.[13]

Results

Basic descriptive statistics are contained in Tables 1 and 2 and are expressed in 1996 Ecus, D marks and pounds sterling. The data refer to CEO total cash compensation from our primary data set. Table 1 considers those CEOs at large companies (i.e. those CEOs in the largest employee size band) and Table 2 contains the mean of CEO pay across the six employee size bands. The most striking feature of the data is the considerable heterogeneity across countries in terms of the cash compensation received by CEOs. CEO pay in large companies in Germany is 421,916 Ecus, and in the UK it is 281,862 Ecus. Ireland has the lowest pay for CEOs, at 104,469 Ecus. This pattern is also more readily seen in Figure 2 which plots CEO compensation (in pounds sterling). In addition, the distribution of European executive pay is not just an artefact of the returns to large companies. The heterogeneity in executive pay is largely unaltered when one considers CEO pay across all size bands (Table 2).

---

[13] We note that it will pick up all country characteristics that are common to the countries going to make up the composite variable Board. This is an inevitable consequence of not having within country variation on board characteristics.

Table 1. The 1996 European distribution of CEO pay (total cash) in large companies

	Executive pay (Ecus)	*Executive pay (DM)*	*Executive pay (Sterling)*
Austria	320,105.84	601,904.50	261,258.50
Belgium	231,027.36	434,255.19	188,540.12
Denmark	302,946.84	569,505.56	247,246.58
Germany	421,916.34	797,000.00	346,070.34
Ireland	104,649.68	196,531.09	85,395.01
Italy	257,599.17	484,027.09	210,260.72
Netherlands	151,988.64	285,841.50	124,081.95
Spain	150,037.41	282,001.41	122,410.98
Switzerland	212,418.30	399,262.91	173,333.33
UK	281,862.75	529,953.94	230,000.00
Total (average)	243,455.23	458,028.32	198,859.75

Source: Remuneration in Europe (1996).

Table 2. The 1996 European distribution of CEO pay (total cash) in all companies

	Executive pay (Ecus)	*Executive pay (DM)*	*Executive pay (Sterling)*
Austria	204,572.95	384,664.59	166,964.85
Belgium	156,750.12	294,638.52	127,922.89
Denmark	233,636.28	439,209.61	190,679.56
Germany	268,660.66	507,500.00	220,364.74
Ireland	113,255.28	212,692.34	92,417.25
Italy	149,557.79	281,018.07	122,073.87
Netherlands	121,354.17	228,227.96	99,072.29
Spain	150,037.41	282,001.41	122,410.98
Switzerland	177,385.62	333,415.23	144,746.67
UK	137,692.40	258,887.11	112,357.00
Total (average)	174,845.58	328,970.42	142,833.21

Source: Remuneration in Europe (1996).

These differences in CEO pay, however, are not wholly attributed to the different structure of European executive compensation. Although there are differences in the structure of CEO compensation, this does not result in a complete harmonization of CEO pay levels across Europe. Indeed, the standard deviation of CEO pay excluding non-cash remuneration (PAY1) is 76,336.32. The standard deviation for the wider pay measure including such non-cash benefits (PAY2) was 84,632.64. So controlling for these wider payment attributes increases (rather than decreases) the variation in our executive compensation measure across the European economies.

Table 3 documents the differences in structural characteristics of CEO pay using the supplementary data from Towers Perrin. In column 1 we compute the total non-cash remuneration as a percentage of total cash remuneration. Recall that total non-cash remuneration is simply the sum of compulsory contributions, voluntary contributions, perquisites and the value of long-term incentives. The average across the available seven countries is approximately 41%. There is variation though: Germany has the lowest ratio (25%) and the UK the highest (67%). Together, this tends to harmonize the value of total compensation of these two countries as can be seen by inspecting Figures 3 and 4. However, as these figures also show (and as noted above) there remain other significant differences in European CEO compensation.

The decomposition of non-cash remuneration into their separate elements is also of some interest. The value of long-term incentives as a percentage of total cash remuneration is highest in the UK. Indeed, in this sample of economies the UK is by far the most extensive user of long-term incentives as a way of rewarding CEOs. The practice is not used to any extent in other European economies.

The econometric results are contained in Table 4, which examines the relationship between executive pay, job level, company size and board structure. Dealing with the job level variables we find that there is a strong positive effect on CEO pay. In all regressions (in columns 1–4) the estimated impact of the job level increases monotonically as one moves to higher corporate positions. The result is not sensitive to the inclusion of size, country

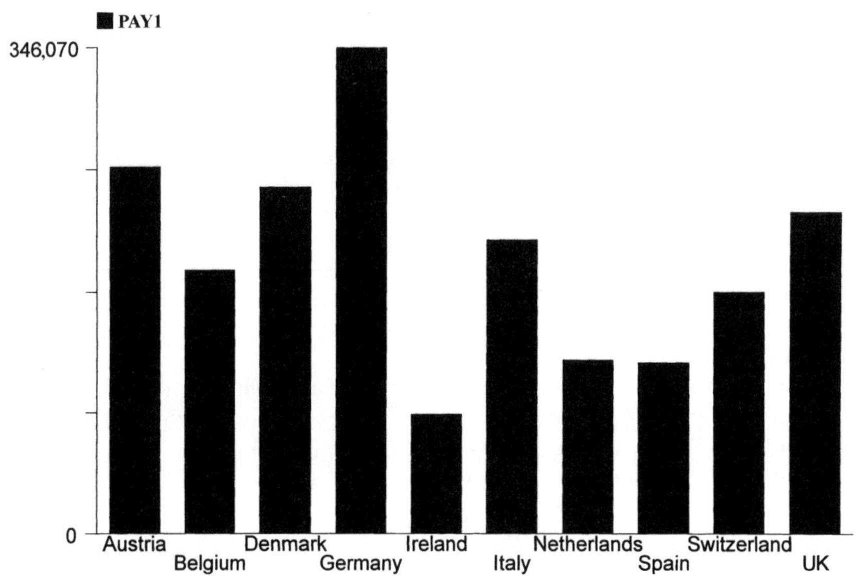

Figure 2. CEO total cash compensation (in pounds sterling).

Table 3. The European distribution of CEO pay characteristics

Country	*Total non-cash remuneration as a % of total cash remuneration*[a]	*Compulsory contributions as a % of total cash remuneration*	*Voluntary contribution as a % of total cash remuneration*	*Perquisites as a % of total cash remuneration*	*Long-term incentives as a % of total cash remuneration*
Austria					
Belgium	56.70	34.90	13.00	8.80	0.00
Denmark					
Germany	25.19	3.00	14.67	7.53	0.00
Ireland					
Italy	50.57	31.49	6.28	7.59	5.21
Netherlands	25.43	0.46	16.83	8.14	0.00
Spain	28.87	3.27	12.00	13.60	0.00
Switzerland	30.71	12.22	10.80	3.00	4.69
UK	66.65	10.20	23.36	8.09	25.00
Total (average)	40.59	13.65	13.85	8.11	4.98

Source: Towers Perrin (1995).

[a]Total non-cash remuneration is the sum of compulsory and voluntary contributions, perquisites and the value of long-term benefits.

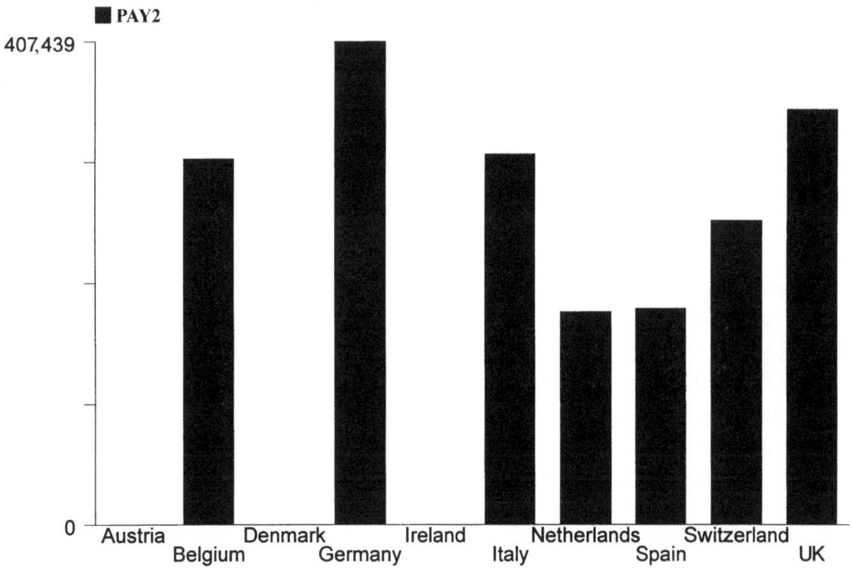

Figure 3. CEO total compensation (in pounds sterling).

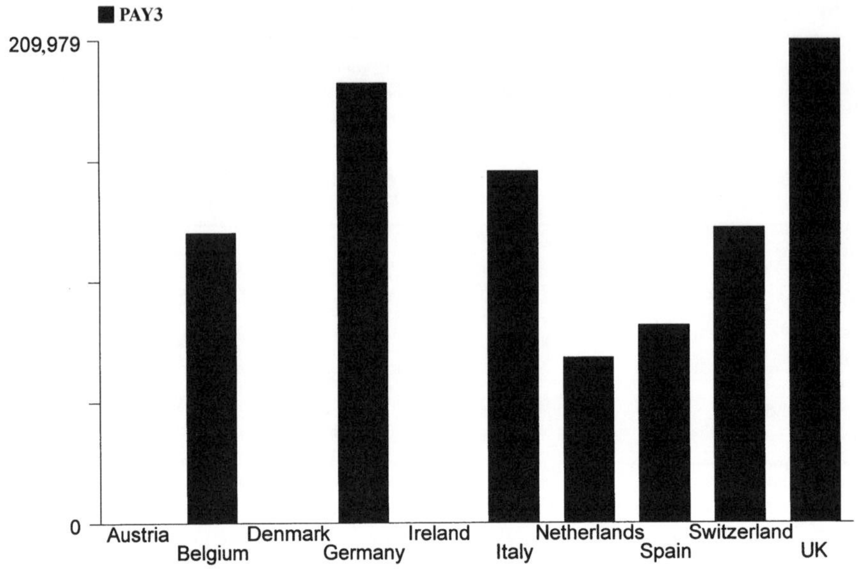

Figure 4. After-tax value of total compensation (in pounds sterling).

or board effects. The return to being the CEO (job level 1) relative to middle managers (job level 5) is 132% (column 3).

Similarly, there is a strong positive correlation between company size and executive pay, as evidenced by the increasing magnitude of the coefficient estimates as one moves from employee band 2 up to the largest employee band 6. The result is obtained after controlling for job position and country specific effects (column 3). The picture that emerges, then, is that executives are rewarded for corporate scale (i.e. large companies pay more). This is consistent with most micro research on executive compensation which reveals that the pay elasticity with respect to company size is in the range 0.2–0.35. Also, our data revealed that more talented individuals (who achieve the top job slot) are also more highly rewarded.

In column 4 we replace the country effects with basic board structure effect. This indicator variable of a type II (2-tier) board system attracts a positive and significant coefficient. The implication is that countries with a 2-tier board system have higher levels of total CEO cash compensation than single board countries. Our prior expectation was that 2-tier boards may have exercised a stronger monitoring function which may have been associated with lower pay.[14] Before we investigate the robustness of this finding to alternative pay measures, we consider various restrictions placed on our basic pay equation.

[14] Of course, this relies on us assuming that the supervisory board is simply putting a halt to management entrenchment. It may well be the case that supervisory board systems realising the superior management talent of their executives may pay them more.

Table 4. Executive pay, job level, company size and country effects

Job level 1	1.409	1.390	1.318	1.343
	(0.084)	(0.069)	(0.042)	(0.061)
Job level 2	1.083	1.076	1.004	1.033
	(0.086)	(0.073)	(0.047)	(0.063)
Job level 3	0.618	0.606	0.535	0.560
	(0.086)	(0.079)	(0.065)	(0.077)
Job level 4	0.295	0.282	0.211	0.241
	(0.077)	(0.065)	(0.040)	(0.062)
Employee band 2		0.074	0.079	0.030
		(0.072)	(0.071)	(0.064)
Employee band 3		0.150	0.159	0.089
		(0.074)	(0.074)	(0.064)
Employee band 4		0.273	0.282	0.212
		(0.077)	(0.074)	(0.066)
Employee band 5		0.374	0.391	0.351
		(0.074)	(0.073)	(0.070)
Employee band 6		0.780	0.693	0.756
		(0.082)	(0.103)	(0.082)
Belgium			–0.060	
			(0.091)	
Denmark			0.239	
			(0.075)	
Germany			0.273	
			(0.079)	
Ireland			–0.521	
			(0.076)	
Italy			–0.120	
			(0.083)	
Netherlands			–0.240	
			(0.075)	
Spain			–0.071	
			(0.095)	
Switzerland			0.084	
			(0.077)	
UK			–0.309	
			(0.117)	
Board				0.325
				(0.039)
Observations	236	236	236	236
R^2	0.6106	0.7225	0.8621	0.7847

Note: Dependent variable is (log) total cash compensation (PAY1).
White (1980) adjusted standard errors reported below coefficient estimates.

Table 5. Statistical restrictions

	Test the effect is jointly zero	*Test the effects are identical*	*R^2 contribution of the effect on pay*
Job level effect	$\alpha_1 = 0$ F(4,217) = 344.55	$\alpha_1 = \ldots = \alpha_4$ F(3,217) = 306.58	0.6106
Company scale effect	$\beta_j = 0$ F(5,217) = 24.57	$\beta_2 = \ldots = \beta_6$ F(4,217) = 29.47	0.1224
Country effects	$\delta_k = 0$ F(9,217) = 56.71	$\delta_2 \ldots = \delta_{10}$ F(8,217) = 63.66	0.2329

Tests in columns 2 and 3 refer to the estimated model:
$y_{ijk} = w + \alpha_1 + \beta_j + \delta_k + \epsilon_{ijk}$ where y is (log) total cash compensation (PAY1).
In column 3 the R^2 are from a regression of y on $\alpha_1, \beta_j, \delta_k$ separately.

Table 5 shows the results of various restrictions on our pay equations. Column 1 provides a test that the joint impact of each pay determinant is zero. In column 2 we test whether the effects of the pay determinants are the same. In the final column we present the R^2 from a regression of executive pay on that determinant of pay only. The row by row results are easy to summarize.[15] The effect of job levels in explaining executive pay is highly significant. A test that the effects are jointly zero is easily rejected (F = 344.55). Moreover, these effects are not identical throughout the corporate hierarchy (F = 306.58). Indeed, this confirms our earlier finding that CEOs are paid significantly more than other levels (e.g. directors) in the corporation. Such a finding is consistent with tournament theories of compensation determination which stress that high pay in the CEO position is needed to motivate executives at lower levels in the company organisation. The effects of job level alone explain 61% of the variation in executive pay. This is an important finding. Managerial talent and the position one holds within a company seem to be a very important factor in shaping company pay outcomes.

In row 2 the effects of company scale are examined. Again, the results indicate that the combined effects of the company size factors on pay cannot be rejected (F = 24.57). In addition, the effects of each size band are not equal (F = 29.47). Finally, the effect of company size alone (excluding job position and country differences) explains 12.24% of the variation in executive pay.

In row 3 we focus on the country effects. Clearly, there are important international differences in explaining European pay outcomes. A test that the country effects are jointly equal to zero is rejected (F = 56.71). Moreover, given

[15] We report the results based on the measure which is simply total cash compensation. The use of wider pay measures did not alter the qualitative results on the size and country effects reported below.

that there are such effects, our results indicate that these are not identical in each country. Indeed, a formal test that the country effects on executive pay are identical is rejected (F = 63.66). Together, these results imply that despite the internationalization of product, capital and labour markets there are still marked national differences which explain executive pay awards across Europe.

Table 6 explores the effect of board type on executive pay further. These regressions do not cater for job effects due to data limitations. First, we should note that regardless of pay measure, the effect of size on executive pay remains strongly positive as before. In column 1 we report the board effect on total CEO cash remuneration. The effect is positive and significant. In column 2 we regress total real compensation (PAY2) on company size and board type. Now the effect has become insignificant. We suspect that this result comes about because of the harmonization between pay rates (particularly Germany and the UK) that occurs when one moves from a cash compensation to a total compensation measure which includes estimates of the value of non-cash components of executive pay. The same conclusion is arrived at when one makes an attempt to control for tax effects (using PAY3) measure. The result here is negative now, but not significant at conventional levels. Overall, we must conclude that countries with two-tier style board structures have an ambiguous relationship with CEO pay. The result, using this macro data, will depend on the type of adjustments that have been made to compensation.

Table 6. CEO pay regressions (alternative measures) on job level and board type

	Total cash compensation (PAY1)	*Total real compensation (PAY2)*	*Total real compensation adjusted (PAY3)*
Employee band 2	0.098	0.059	0.067
	(0.109)	(0.085)	(0.127)
Employee band 3	0.252	0.135	0.143
	(0.111)	(0.093)	(0.126)
Employee band 4	0.380	0.178	0.225
	(0.130)	(0.111)	(0.158)
Employee band 5	0.488	0.337	0.345
	(0.131)	(0.096)	(0.132)
Employee band 6	0.966	0.654	0.732
	(0.104)	(0.090)	(0.125)
Board	0.392	–0.024	–0.123
	(0.072)	(0.063)	(0.086)
Observations	48	33	33
R^2	0.653	0.570	0.488

Note: Regression of different chief executive pay measures on employee band size and board type. White (1980) adjusted standard errors reported below coefficient estimates.

Conclusions

This chapter has examined differences in executive pay across a sample of 10 European economies. The research was motivated by the paucity of cross-country evidence on the level and structure of executive pay. To aid our analysis we have used a unique data set which has information on executive pay, classified by job level, company size and country. Our international comparison of executive pay has used macro data assembled for each country by remuneration specialists. Micro-data on individual firms across these economies were not available.

Our main results indicated that there are many complex drivers of European executive pay. Not least are the positive influences of managerial talent which we proxied by job position and corporate size. Our results indicated that both job level and company size were important statistical determinants of European pay. Indeed, together these variables explained much of the variation in executive pay.

We examined whether increased European integration and the effects of factor price equalisation resulted in executive compensation that was more equal for individuals with similar abilities and characteristics. If such a process were complete, then after controlling for individual factors we might expect the country specific effects should be negligible. Our results indicated a significant role for country effects in shaping executive pay. Factor price equalization has not yet resulted in similar executive pay outcomes across Europe for individuals working in a given job level, with similar talents, or in the same size company. However, a strong test of this might require micro data.

We also exploited the level and structure of pay according to the governance system in operation. Having classified the European economies into governance types I and II, we found that the effect of boards on executive pay was ambiguous. Economies with type II board structures had higher total cash compensation for executives. However, once the effect of other components of compensation had been accounted for then the correlation between board type and CEO pay was not significant. We found that the board effect depended on how the executive compensation variable was defined.

Our analysis contributes to the wider debate about executive pay in Europe and the governance mechanisms that shape it. Our analysis here has taken place using essentially macro data. Accordingly, we have provided a broad picture of the European scene. We are, however, acutely aware that such data are prone to many methodological problems that, in the context of this paper, cannot be addressed. An immediate problem to square up to is the role of individual firms in setting pay. A worthy future project would take individual company level data from a set of European economies and then test what factors are most important in explaining executive pay. This would have the very real advantage of being able to discriminate between board and governance effects by having within country variation on such variables.

Acknowledgements

We would like to thank Andy Cosh, Michael Lemmon, Steve Machin, Todd Milbourn, Kevin Murphy, Simon Peck and participants at the Stern School, New York University conference on executive compensation and shareholder value for helpful comments and suggestions. Sourafel Girma was kind enough to collect some of the British data and Ulrike Grasshoff and Annett Klein the German data. We are grateful to the Sonderforschungsbereich 373 at Humboldt-University Berlin and the UK Economic and Social Research Council for supporting this research. Views, errors and omissions are, of course, the authors' responsibility.

Appendix

Table A1. The distributions of companies for the European pay comparisons

Countries	*Number of companies*
Austria	175
Belgium	49
Denmark	353
Germany	647
Ireland	182
Italy	350
Netherlands	173
Spain	351
Switzerland	172
UK	394
Total	2,846

Source: Remuneration in Europe. Supplied by the European Independents Remuneration Network (1997). The data refers to 1996.

Table A2. The classification of European economies to type I and type II board structures

Country	*Governance type*	*Personal income tax*
Austria	Type II	
Belgium	Type I	0.59
Denmark	Type II	
Germany	Type II	0.53
Ireland	Type I	
Italy	Type I	0.51
Netherlands	Type II	0.60
Spain	Type I	0.53
Switzerland	Type II	0.50
UK	Type I	0.40

Sources: Governance types: Korn Ferry International.
Personal income tax: Abowd and Bognanno (1993) Table 2.6 page 91.

References

Abowd, J. and M. Bognanno (1993). International differences in executive and managerial compensation. In: R. Freeman and L. Katz (eds), *Differences and Changes in Wage Structures.* University of Chicago Press, Chicago, 67–103.

Alcouffe, A. (1998). Gouvernement d'entreprise et contrôle interne. Actes du séminaire, Ecole de Printemps en Economie et Gestion 1998. ESSEC – Ecole Polytechnique, Ecole des Mines, Cergy Pontoise, 25/26 mai, 1998.

Angel, P.O. and V.S. Fumas (1997). The compensation of Spanish executives. A test of a managerial talent allocation model. *International Journal of Industrial Organization*, **15**, 511–532.

Baums, T. (1994). Stellungsnahme. *Zeitschrift für Bankrecht und Bankwirtschaft*, **6**, 94.

Biehler, B. and P. Liepmann (1988). Personelle Verbindungen und intersektorale Finanzbeziehungen zwischen den größten deutschen Unternehmen. *Jahrbuch fuer Nationaloekonomie und Statistik*, **204**, 48–68.

Cadbury, A. (1992). *Final Report of the Committee on the Financial Aspects of Corporate Governance.* London, Gee Publishing.

Charkham, J.P. (1995). *Keeping Good Company: A Study of Corporate Governance in Five Countries.* Oxford, Oxford University Press.

Conyon, M.J. (1997). Corporate governance and executive compensation. *International Journal of Industrial Organization*, **15**, 493–509.

Conyon, M.J., P. Gregg and S. Machin (1995). Taking care of business: executive compensation in the UK. *Economic Journal*, **105**, 704–715.

Conyon, M.J. and S.I. Peck (1998). Recent developments on UK corporate governance. In: Buxton, A., P. Chapman and P. Temple (eds.), *Britain's Economic Performance.* London & New York, 253–277.

Cosh, A. and A. Hughes (1997). Executive remuneration, executive dismissal and institutional shareholdings. *International Journal of Industrial Organization*, **15**, 469-492.

Crystal, G. (1992). *In Search of Success: The Overcompensation of American Executives.* W.W. Norton and Co., New York and London.

Eriksson, T. (1996). *Executive Compensation and Tournament Theory: Empirical Tests on Danish Data.* Aarhus Business School mimeograph.

Eriksson, T. and M. Lausten (1996). *Managerial Pay and Firm Performance – Danish Evidence.* Aarhus Business School mimeograph.

Grasshoff, U. and J. Schwalbach (1997). *Corporate Restructuring, Downsizing and Managerial Compensation.* Humboldt-University Berlin, Institute of Management, working paper no. 97–2.

Greenbury, R. (1995). *Report of the Committee on Executive Remuneration.* Gee Publishing, London.

Hampel, R. (1998). *Committee on Corporate Governance: Final Report (Hampel Committee Report).* Gee Publishing, London.

Hart, O. (1995). Corporate governance: some theory and implications. *Economic Journal*, **105**, 678–689.

Jensen, M.C. and K.J. Murphy (1990). Performance pay and top management incentives. *Journal of Political Economy,* **98**, 225–264.

Jensen, M.C. (1993). The modern industrial revolution, exit, and the failure of internal control mechanisms. *Journal of Finance*, **48**, 831–880.

Kaplan, S. (1994). Top executive rewards and firm performance: a comparison of Japan and the United States. *Journal of Political Economy*, **102(3)**, 510–46.

Korn Ferry International (1996). *European Boards of Directors Study.* Korn/Ferry International, London.

Lazear, E.P. and S. Rosen (1981). Rank-order tournaments as optimum labor contracts. *Journal of Political Economy*, **89**, 841–864.

Lazear, E.P. (1989). Pay equality and industrial politics. *Journal of Political Economy*, **97**, 561–580.

Lazear, E.P. (1995). *Personnel Economics.* The MIT Press, Cambridge, MA.

Main, B.G.M., A. Bruce and T. Buck (1996). Total board remuneration and company performance. *Economic Journal*, **106**, 1627–44.

Mayer, C. (1996). *Corporate Governance, Competition and Performance.* Economics Department, OECD, Paris.

Murphy, K.J. (1998). Executive compensation. In: O. Ashenfelter and D. Card (eds.), *Handbook of Labor Economics*, **3**, forthcoming.

Nickell, S.J. (1995). *The Performance of Companies: The Relationship Between the External Environment, Management Strategies and Corporate Performance.* Basil Blackwell, Oxford.

P-E International (1997). *Remuneration in Europe.* The European Independents Network.

Pfannschmidt, A. (1995). Mehrfachmandate in deutschen Unternehmen. *Zeitschrift für Betriebswirtschaft*, **65**, 177–203.

Rosen, S. (1992). Contracts and the market for executives. In: L. Wernin and H. Wijlander (eds). *Contract Economics.* Basil Blackwell, Oxford.

Schmalensee, R. (1985). Do markets differ much? *American Economic Review*, **75**, 341–51.

Schwalbach, J. and U. Grasshof (1997). Managervergütung und Unternehmenserfolg. *Zeitschrift für Betriebswirtschaft*, **67**, 203–217.

Towers Perrin (1996). *World-wide Total Remuneration.* New York.

BRIAN J. HALL
Harvard University and NBER

3. A better way to pay CEOs?

Introduction

Managerial incentives can no longer be understood without a solid understanding of stock options. Stock option grants have increased dramatically in the past 15 years or so. For example, the average CEO stock option grant (valued at Black-Scholes and in inflation adjusted 1994 dollars) increased from \$155 thousand to \$1.2 million between 1980 and 1994, representing an almost 700% increase. Moreover, for the largest publicly traded companies, stock option grants are now larger on average than salary and bonus combined, and more than 90% of all CEOs now hold stock options (Hall and Liebman, 1998).

This dramatic increase in executive stock options represents a fundamental change in corporate governance, and it raises a number of questions that are not well understood. How have the incentives of top managers changed? Is it the stock or flow of stock options that matter? How do the incentives from stock ownership differ from those of stock option holdings? Do stock options have large downside risks? If so, under what conditions? What are the implications of this? Why has there been such a large increase in stock option grants? Finally, are there better ways to pay top managers?

In this chapter, I address some of these difficult questions by discussing them in the context of my recent research (Hall and Liebman, 1998; Hall, 1998).

Managerial incentives and agency costs

Because of agency problems (Jensen and Meckling, 1976), corporate governance and incentive problems are enormous in large publicly traded companies. It is extremely difficult in very large organizations to align the incentives of managers with the goals of owners. Ownership of such companies is quite diffuse and the large size of the companies makes it difficult for CEOs to purchase a large proportion of the firm's equity. As a result, managers often

---

This paper was prepared for the conference on *Executive Compensation and Shareholder Value: Theory and Evidence*, at New York University's Salomon Center, Stern School of Business, October 24, 1997.

J. Carpenter and D. Yermack (eds.), Executive Compensation and Shareholder Value, 35–46.

take actions and make decisions that are at odds with shareholder value maximization. Such actions include, for example, 'empire building' and the purchase of expensive[1] and unnecessary perks such as corporate jets. Moreover, the evidence that managers use their position to pursue private benefits at the expense of owners is quite extensive. Agency costs are large and pervasive.

The agency problem can be mitigated through board monitoring of the CEO, but monitoring is a blunt and typically ineffective solution to the agency problem. There are an almost unlimited number of actions a CEO can take and they are highly complex. Boards typically do not know what *ex ante* actions maximize firm value (which is one of the reasons they hired a CEO), and even if they did, verifying actions *ex post* is extremely difficult. If one takes the analysis back one step, why should we believe that the board has the right incentives to monitor the CEO in the first place? Even the best monitoring in large corporations is unlikely to solve, or perhaps even substantially reduce, the agency problem.

The most direct way to reduce agency problems is through high-powered incentive schemes; that is, by tying CEO pay very closely to shareholder value creation. In very large corporations this is difficult to do, because typical swings in the market value of large corporations are quite large relative to the wealth of CEOs. For example, imagine a company with a market value of $10 billion. A 30% change in the market value (which is approximately equal to the annual standard deviation of returns of the largest companies) represents a $3 billion change in shareholder wealth. If CEO wealth changed by even 10% of that value, CEO wealth would increase or decline by $300 million. Very few CEOs have enough wealth to make this type of contract even remotely feasible. Moreover, even if contracts with such large swings in CEO wealth could be written, it is not clear that such contracts would be optimal given CEO risk aversion (Haubrich, 1994).[2]

The insights of agency theory in the context of large, publicly traded corporations underscores both the importance and the difficulty of aligning CEO pay with shareholder value. Such alignment is important because the alternative mechanism of control, monitoring, is likely to be fairly ineffective given that diffuse shareholders have neither the ability nor the incentives to closely monitor CEO actions and decisions. Such alignment is difficult because wealth-constrained CEOs will invariably own a small fraction of the largest companies, making it difficult to get CEOs to 'think like owners'. During the past 15 years, boards have attempted to mitigate this problem by making CEOs into effective owners by granting them stock options on a yearly basis. In the remainder of this paper, I will describe this phenomenon, showing how the explosion in stock option grants has succeeded in better aligning pay and

---

[1] See Shleifer and Vishny, 1997.

[2] If incentives are too high-powered, the resulting large swings in CEO wealth may lead CEOs to avoid high-risk, high-return projects that are desirable from the perspective of diversified shareholders. That is, CEOs may price idiosyncratic risk (Hall and Liebman, 1998).

performance. I then analyze some ways in which current compensation practices can be improved.

Some stylized facts about CEO pay to performance

What creates pay to performance?

The most remarkable fact about CEO incentives is that virtually all of the pay to performance relationship comes from the fact that CEOs hold millions of dollars of company stock and stock options, which change in value as the value of the firm changes. That is, the annual revaluation of CEO stock and stock option holdings swamp the annual changes in their salary and bonus.

For example, virtually all studies find that the elasticity of CEO compensation with respect to firm value is approximately 0.1–0.15.[3] Hall and Liebman (1998) estimated a slightly higher elasticity of about 0.24 for the late 1980s and early 1990s. Although this estimate is higher than previous estimates, it still implies a relatively small relationship between CEO pay and firm performance. For example, this estimate implies that increasing a firm's market value by an additional 10% during the year increases a CEO's salary and bonus by 2.4%, which is equal to about $25,000 for a CEO with a salary and bonus of slightly more than $1 million per year (about the median salary and bonus of the CEOs in our sample of large companies).

For the same change in firm value, revaluations of CEO stock and stock options are about 50 times larger. That is, while a 10% increase in firm value increases salary and bonus by about $25,000 at the median, it increases the value of the median CEO's stock and stock options by about $1.25 million. Thus, if 'compensation' is defined more broadly to include all changes in CEO wealth (direct pay plus changes in the value of CEO stock and stock option holdings) then the pay to performance relationship rises by a factor of 50.[4]

The fact that stock and stock option revaluations represent about 98% of the pay to performance relationship suggests that annual changes in salary and bonus are only the tip of the iceberg in terms of total pay to performance. Of course, CEOs may give disproportionate weight to annual changes in salary and bonus, but the fact that salary and bonus changes are so small (in relative terms) suggests that CEOs who pay close attention to their overall compensation package will realize that it is their stock and stock option holdings that tie their fortunes to the fortunes of the companies they manage.

---

3 See Rosen (1992).

4 Likewise, we find that elasticity of pay with respect to firm value is approximately 4, instead of 0.24, when CEO compensation is broadened to include stock and stock option revaluations.

Measuring CEO pay to performance

As discussed earlier, in the largest publicly traded companies it is very difficult to generate large swings in CEO wealth relative to swings in firm value, simply because the companies are so large. In a seminal article, Jensen and Murphy (1990a) used data from the 1970s and early 1980s and showed that total CEO wealth changed by only $3.25 cents for every $1,000 change in shareholder value, concluding that CEOs are essentially paid like bureaucrats (1990b). Hall and Liebman (1998) revisited this issue and found that this measure of sensitivity essentially doubled between 1980 and 1994; on a size-adjusted basis, this measure of sensitivity quadrupled over the same period.[5] While this represents a substantial increase in sensitivity, changes in CEO wealth remain small relative to dollar changes in firm value.

A point we emphasize in our paper, however, is that because these companies are so large, our estimated level of sensitivity implies very large dollar swings in CEO wealth in response to typical changes in firm value. This is the case simply because the companies are so large that typical changes in firm value are often in the hundreds of millions, or even billions, of dollars. For example, the standard deviation of annual firm returns is approximately 32% for the firms in our sample. A one standard deviation increase (decrease) in firm value increases (decreases) the median CEO's wealth by about $4 million, which hardly seems small. So typical swings in CEO wealth are small when measured against changes in firm value, but are large in absolute dollar terms.

As another example, we calculated all of the annual returns for the firms in our sample (which included roughly half of the largest firms during the past 25 years), and then ranked the returns to form deciles. For example, a 10th percentile return is –27.6%, implying that 10% of firm years have annual returns of –27.6% or less. The decile cutoff at the 90th percentile is 47.9%. We then imposed each of the decile returns on the contracts (their stock and stock option holdings) for all of our CEOs, which produced a distribution of total compensation for each CEO at each decile return. For example, at the 10th percentile return, the median CEO in our sample loses about $435,000 – that is, the negative changes in the value of stock and stock options are larger in absolute value than the CEO's total direct pay, which is assumed to be constant. When a 90th percentile return is imposed on all of the contracts, the median CEO makes about $8.5 million, most of which comes from positive revaluation of stock and stock option holdings. Put a bit crudely, for the typical CEO in our sample, there is about a $9 million difference in pay in moving from a very bad firm performance to an excellent performance.

Moreover, the relationship between pay and performance has increased

---

[5] The Jensen and Murphy sensitivity measure has a strong, negative relationship with firm size. Since the Fortune 500 firms became much larger during this 15 year period, it became increasingly harder for the CEOs of these companies to increase this sensitivity since its natural tendency is to decrease as firm size increases.

dramatically since 1980. For example, in 1980, CEOs received about $242,000 for a 10th percentile performance and $1.8 million for a 90th percentile performance, which represents an increase of only $1.6 million (again at the median), much smaller than the commensurate $9 million difference for 1994. The rise in stock option awards during the past 15 years has dramatically increased the relationship between CEO pay, defined broadly, and firm performance.

Stock options and incentives

The previous analysis suggests that when it comes to monetary incentives, equity-based pay is now the primary driver of pay to performance. The fact remains, however, that the incentives provided by options are not well understood, either by executives or the boards that grant the options to the CEOs. Perhaps this is to be expected. In order to understand the incentives provided by stock options, it is necessary to understand the value of those options, but determining the value of options is not so intuitive. Indeed, option valuation is sufficiently complex that two economists, Robert Merton and Myron Scholes, were recently awarded the Nobel Prize for developing the framework for valuing options.

In a recent paper (Hall, 1998) I analyzed the pay to performance incentives created by executive stock options, which I summarize here. The most confusing feature about executive stock options is their downside risk. Indeed, it is commonly argued that the difference between stock and stock options is that stock has upside potential and downside risk, but stock options have only upside potential and no downside risk. This is not the case. Indeed, if the proper thought experiment is conducted, then it is the case that stock options have more downside risk than stock. Explanation on this point is necessary.

The view that stock options have limited downside risk rests, at least in part, on the fact that, when the stock price changes, the value of one option changes by less than the value of one share of stock changes. That is, an option's delta (the change in option value for a derivative change in the share price) is less than one, and falls as the stock price pushes an option contract further out of the money. While this is correct, it does not imply that options have little downside risk. Options have value. As the price of the stock falls, the value of options also falls. The only question is by how much?

It is instructive to perform some analysis with options that have characteristics closely matching the typical CEO stock option grant of a typical Fortune 500 company. The typical stock option grant is at the money (the exercise price is equal to the current stock price) and has a duration of 10 years. Fortune 500 companies have dividend rates of about 3.5% and stock prices with annual standard deviations of about 32% (both are medians). I assume a 6% risk free rate, which approximates the 10 year bond rate. Under those assumptions, an 'at the money' option has a delta of about 0.55 – that is, the value of one option changes by 55% of the value of one share of stock.

The key, however, is this: for the same *ex ante* value transfer to the CEO, a company can give a greater number of stock options than stock shares because each option is worth less than each share. In fact, a company can give about three times as many options as shares for the same *ex ante* value transfer to the CFO. More importantly, the greater sensitivity induced by a larger number of shares more than offsets the lower sensitivity per option (relative to stock). As shown at the top of Table 1, for the typical stock option, a company can transfer about three at the money options for every transfer of one share. Since each option has a delta that is about 0.55, the total sensitivity of options is about 1.7 (about 3 times 0.55) times higher than that of stock. This is the leverage effect of stock options as a compensation tool. The same *ex ante* transfer of options has more sensitivity than the equivalent value of stock shares.

By extension, the same *ex ante* transfer of out of the money options has greater sensitivity than at the money options.[6] An option with an exercise price that is 50% above the stock price is worth only about one-fourth of one share of stock, which implies that a company can give about four options (4.2 to be more precise) for every share (see Table 1). Since each out of the money option has a delta of about 0.45, the total sensitivity of such an out of the money option is 1.88 times larger than that of stock. Out of the money options have even greater sensitivity than at the money options. Strikingly, this includes downside as well as upside sensitivity.

An example (example 1 in Table 1) will illustrate the leverage effect of options. The benchmark transfer to the CEO is $1 million worth of stock. The CEO is granted 1 million shares of stock worth $1 each. If the stock price increases by 25%, from $1 to $1.25, the CEO realizes a gain of $0.25 million. Now imagine that the CEO is given one dollar's worth of at the money options instead. Even though the value of each option rises by less (the delta over this range of stock prices is about 0.57), the CEO is granted about three times as many (since each option is worth about one-third of a share). The total sensitivity of options is therefore 1.73 times higher than that of stock and the CEO now realizes a gain of $0.43 million rather than $0.25 million.

The gain to a CEO holding out of the money options is even higher, as shown in column 3 of example 1 in Table 1. In this case, the CEO holds four times as many options as shares, each with a delta of 0.48 for a total sensitivity that is twice that of shares. The CEO thus gains $0.5 million (a 50% gain) when the stock price increases by 25%.

The same basic logic applies to downward movements in the stock price (as shown in example 2 of Table 1), although the leverage effect of options is slightly smaller in the downward direction since option deltas fall as the stock price falls. (Out of the money deltas are lower than deltas for at the money

---

6 See Dial and Murphy (1995) for an example of this. General dynamics replaced out of the money options with the same value as the money options, which reduced sensitivity rather than increasing it.

Table 1. The larger pay to performance sensitivity of executive stock options relative to stock [Example: CEO receives $1 million of stock or options. The stock price is initially $1 per share.]

	Stock	*At the money options* ($P_E = P$)	*Out of the money options* ($P_E = 1.5*P$)
# of shares/options (in millions)	1	3.06	4.17
Times delta (change in the value of one share or one option per $1 change in stock price)	1	0.55	0.45
Equals sensitivity (in millions)	1	1.67	1.88
Example 1: Increase in share price from $1 to $1.25			
# of shares/options (millions)	1	3.06	4.17
Times delta (over range)	1	0.57	0.48
Equals sensitivity (millions)	1	1.73	2.00
Times price change	$0.25	$0.25	$0.25
Equals total change in value	$0.25 million	$0.43 million	$0.50 million
Example 2: Decrease in share price from $1 to $0.75			
# of shares/options (millions)	1	3.06	4.17
Times delta (over range)	1	0.51	0.41
Equals sensitivity (millions)	1	1.56	1.71
Times price change	–$0.25	–$0.25	–$0.25
Equals total change in value	–$0.25 million	–$0.39 million	–$0.43 million

Source: Hall (1998)
Note: assume that the risk free rate of return is 6%, the duration of the options is 10 years, the dividend rate is 3.5% and the annual standard deviation of stock returns is 32%

options, which are lower than deltas for in the money options). If the stock price falls from $1.00 to $0.75, a CEO holding $1 million worth of stock loses $0.25 million while a CEO holding $1 million worth of at the money options loses $0.39 million, a loss that is 1.56 times larger. A CEO holding $1 million worth of out of the money options loses even more – $0.43 million. The key conclusion is that, for the same value transfer to the CEO, options have greater pay to performance sensitivity than stock and out of the money options have greater sensitivity than at the money options. And this is true for downside as well as upside sensitivity.[7]

Changing the way CEOs are paid

The granting of stock options represents a convenient method for creating high-powered financial incentives for top managers. In theory boards could use changes in direct pay, salary and bonus, to motivate managers, but unless there are dramatic changes in the way that boards operate, it is unlikely that salary and bonus will become a tool for the type of high powered incentives that result from executive stock option holdings.

The main problem is that high powered incentives require large upside swings and large downside swings, and, in the case of salary and bonus, each is resisted for a different reason. On the upside, very large bonuses are resisted by what Jensen and Murphy (1990a,b) call implicit regulation. Executive pay is a politically sensitive topic. Large bonuses tend to attract the attention of the media and the public and invite criticism, even if the bonuses are orders of magnitude smaller than the gain to shareholders. Stock option gains, while still inviting some criticism, seem to be less controversial. As one compensation consultant told me, "Last year, [a particular CEO] made about $10 million in stock option appreciation, which was his reward for spectacular company performance. It would be inconceivable too for the board to give him the equivalent $10 million in year-end bonus."

On the downside, large decreases in salary or bonuses are resisted by CEOs. Boards are often quite friendly with the CEOs and find it hard to impose large decreases in compensation on their friends. Moreover, compensation consultants, who can be fired for giving unwelcome advice, are reluctant to push for large decreases in compensation. The idea that the board would impose a multi-million dollar negative bonus on the CEO for poor company performance, which is effectively what happens when the CEO holds stock and stock options and the firm's price declines substantially, is not something that is even considered in most boardrooms today.

---

[7] The downside risk of stock options is not always higher than that of stock. The total downside risk of stock and stock options, where total downside risk is defined as the loss from the stock price falling to zero, is trivially the same for both stock and stock options since the ex ante values of each are the same. In both cases, the CEO loses the entire $1 million. But over the most relevant regions for price declines, downward stock option sensitivity is greater than stock sensitivity. See Hall (1998) for details.

It is therefore hard to imagine that salary and bonus will ever provide the type of high-powered incentives that come automatically from stock option holdings. Options represent a nice vehicle for aligning the incentives of owners and managers. There are, however, a number of ways in which current compensation plans can be improved.

Premium options and indexed options

The previous analysis suggests that out of the money options, sometimes called premium options, have greater pay to performance sensitivity (over most regions of stock price movements) than standard options for the same *ex ante* value transfer to the CEO. For companies eager to increase CEO pay to performance, this makes out of the money options an attractive alternative to standard options; they have greater downside and much greater upside sensitivity. Hall (1998) conducted simulations on the actual CEO contracts by counterfactually assuming that all options were originally issued at an exercise price that is 50% out of the money. The analysis suggests that, if such a policy were adopted, pay to performance sensitivity would rise by 15–38%, depending on what stock price region is examined.

Indexed options represent another attractive alternative to the current practice of issuing only at the money options to top executives. Indexed options have an exercise price that rises over time with some market index – for example, the S&P 500. Indexed options, thus, have the obvious advantage that CEOs are not rewarded or punished for overall movements in the stock market. Because the (expected) future exercise price is higher than the current stock price, indexed options are leveraged in a way that is similar to premium options. An executive can only make a profit on an indexed option if the price rises above a certain hurdle, in this case the increase in the S&P 500. Since each option is therefore worth substantially less than an at the money option, an executive can be granted many more of them. So, for the same transfer to the CEO, the pay to performance sensitivity of indexed options is higher than the sensitivity of at the money options (see Hall 1998).

It would be extreme to suggest the complete abandonment of at the money options in favor of granting only premium options or indexed options. Many risk averse CEOs would resist (and therefore demand a premium for accepting) the complete replacement of their at the money options with the more leveraged (and therefore riskier) premium or indexed options (all with the same Black-Scholes valuation). Nevertheless, the almost complete absence of premium or indexed options seems puzzling given their striking advantages in terms of pay to performance.

An interesting feature of premium and indexed options is that they are likely to be popular with both shareholders and the public, at least relative to the current practice of granting only at the money options. With premium options, it is clear that CEOs have to substantially raise the share price before they receive any payoff. With indexed options, CEOs only make a profit if their company's stock price performance beats the market (which rises over time). Both types of options raise the hurdle. For those who believe that current executive pay practices give CEOs too much of a free ride, raising the performance hurdle with premium or indexed options would represent an attractive alternative to current pay practices.

Scoring the CEO's option package

As stated earlier, a key drawback of options is that their valuation is complex. Indeed, in some cases, it seems that CEOs have no idea how much their options are worth. More importantly, they do not understand how much their option packages change with changes in the value of their companies. Indeed, I believe it is the case that boards, and many academics, do not understand the incentive properties of option holdings. This presents a serious problem: if options are not understood, how can they provide the right incentives?

Boards can improve their compensation and incentive policies by adopting the formal practice of valuing their executive's options each quarter. This quarterly 'scoring' could be coupled with a straightforward sensitivity analysis, which shows the executive how much his or her option package changes with various changes, upwards and downwards, in the company's stock price. If such a practice were adopted, I suspect that many CEOs would be shocked at how much their stock option portfolio changes in response to changes in market value. Many CEOs tend to focus on their salary and bonus, which change by only trivial amounts relative to stock and stock option revaluations. A quarterly scoring of the value of their stock options would appropriately refocus their attention on the main task for which they have been hired, creating value for the owners of the company.

Maintaining incentive alignment

The goal of incentive-based pay is to align the incentives of managers with the goals of owners. Such alignment often conflicts with the preferences of CEOs. One CEO of an investment company used this argument to convince the board to let him sell off much of his stock: "We would never advise our clients to be so undiversified. So why should I be so undiversified?" The answer is simple: the goal of CEO compensation is not to optimize the risk of the CEO portfolios. The goal is to align the CEO's incentives with those of shareholders; these goals are in conflict. A good incentive contract will generally have the feature that the CEO will want to shed some of the company's risk. There is no escaping the problem that high-powered incentives put some CEO wealth at risk, which is undesirable for risk-averse CEOs who want their portfolios to be better diversified.

CEOs can hedge their positions in their companies by selling their stock or by exercising their options for cash. Indeed, Ofek and Yermack (1997) argue that CEOs can, and do, hedge some of their risk in this way. This is counterproductive to the goal of equity-based pay. There are two possible responses to this, both of which would be an improvement over current practices. The first would be to put more restrictions on the selling of stock and the cashing in of stock options. In the case of stock options, this would imply coupling stock option awards with longer vesting periods.

The second is to establish guidelines or goals for the overall amount of stock and stock options that CEOs must hold. Many companies have established ownership guidelines in recent years. For example, CEOs are expected to hold stock that is valued at four or five times their salary and bonus. Although these guidelines are a step in the right direction, the contain a major flaw: they do not include stock option holdings. Indeed, because of this, CEOs have an incentive to exercise their stock options and use the profits to buy stock but, as this analysis suggests, this essentially deleverages their position in the company, which reduces the alignment of their incentives with those of shareholders. The policy implication of this is obvious: the ownership guidelines should be revised to include stock options as well as stock, which will require an appropriate upward adjustment in the ratio (since stock options will now count, making it easier to reach the ratio).

Conclusion

In the end, the explosion in CEO stock option awards during the past 15 years has had the desired effect of creating a stronger link between CEO pay and firm performance. While this is an important step in the right direction, I believe there are a variety of ways in which current compensation practices can be improved. In particular, I have argued that both premium options and indexed options have important pay to performance advantages relative to the current practice of issuing only at the money options. Given the leverage benefits of premium and indexed options, their almost complete absence as a compensation tool for top executives is a bit of a puzzle.

In addition, I believe that incentives would be improved significantly if boards adopted the practice of valuing or 'scoring' the CEO's option packages on a quarterly basis. Pay to performance incentives are undermined to the extent that the executives they are meant to motivate do not understand them. Finally, compensation practices would be improved if boards better dealt with the tension between a CEO's desire to hedge risk and the shareholder's goal of maintaining incentive alignment over a CEO's career. Lengthening stock option vesting periods and changing the ownership guidelines to include options represent two straightforward ways to maintain such alignment over time.

References

Dial, J. and K.J. Murphy (1995). Incentives, downsizing and value creation at general dynamics, *Journal of Financial Economics,* **37**, 261–314.

Hall, B.J. (1998). The Pay to Performance Incentives of Executive Stock Options. NBER Working Paper 6674, August.

Hall, B.J. and J.B. Liebman (1998). Are CEOs Really Paid Like Bureaucrats? *Quarterly Journal of Economics*, **113**, 653–691.

Haubrich, J.G. (1994). Risk aversion, performance pay and the principal agent problem. *Journal of Political Economy*, **102**, 258–276.

Jensen, M.C. and W.M. Meckling (1976). Theory of the firm: managerial behavior, agency costs and ownership structure, *Journal of Financial Economics*, **3**, 305–360.

Jensen, M.C. and K.J. Murphy (1990a). CEO incentives – it's not how much you pay, but how. *Harvard Business Review.*

Jensen, M.C. and K.J. Murphy (1990b). Performance pay and top-management incentives. *Journal of Political Economy*, **97**, 225–264.

Ofek, E. and D. Yermack (1997). *Taking Stock: Does Equity-Based Compensation Increase Manager's Ownership?* Unpublished draft.

Rosen, S. (1992). Contracts and the market for executives. In L. Werin and H. Wijkander (eds), *Contract Economics*, Oxford: Blackwell, 181–211.

Shleifer, A. and R. Vishny (1997). A survey of corporate governance. *Journal of Finance*, **52**, 737–783.

TODD T. MILBOURN
London Business School

4. The winner-takes-all: an alternative view of CEO incentives*

INTRODUCTION

The research on executive remuneration offered by Kaplan, Conyon and Schwalbach[1] and Hall certainly provides for interesting reading. In fact, each contributes positively to our understanding of executive pay packages in practice. Instead of offering a comment on each paper individually, however, I employ an alternative strategy. When these papers are considered jointly, they provide a platform that is well suited to consider international contracting issues, as well as investigate an alternative model of managerial incentives. To this end, I suggest three questions below and attempt to provide preliminary answers by drawing upon the findings of the authors' collective work.

First, what do these recent data reveal about the current state of international pay? Second, are standard empirical tests of executive remuneration accounting for all the incentives offered to executives? That is, are there additional managerial incentive effects introduced by implicit managerial tournaments? Lastly, what can we conclude about the future of executive pay in the global arena?

Why focus on these issues? In all fairness, I am (more than) slightly biased toward these topics based on my own research interests. However, I believe they arise quite naturally from within the collective framework of Kaplan, Conyon and Schwalbach, and Hall. Their findings that are relevant to the questions posed above are briefly summarized next.

Among other things, Kaplan provides a cross-country synthesis of some of his earlier work on Chief Executive Officer (CEO) remuneration across Germany, Japan and the USA. Both anecdotal evidence and corporate contracting theory would suggest that the capital market-dominated financial

* This is a comment on papers by Kaplan, Conyon and Schwalbach and Hall, which were presented at the 1997 NYU Conference on Executive Compensation.

[1] I will focus my comments on their paper entitled *European Differences in Executive Pay and Corporate Governance.* I acknowledge the fact that the authors chose to present a companion paper at the conference and apologize to them for the paucity of comments on that work.

J. Carpenter and D. Yermack (eds.), Executive Compensation and Shareholder Value, 47–52.

system of the USA would engender a significantly stronger relationship between CEO pay and firm performance. However, what Kaplan uncovers is that, on average, the sensitivity of CEO cash pay to firm performance is (statistically) equivalent across these three countries. This evidence will allow us to address the first question regarding international pay packages.

Next, Conyon and Schwalbach utilize macro-level compensation data to explore the variation in the levels of managerial pay across Europe.[2] Their data, although slightly constrained by their aggregate nature, are quite interesting as they span several managerial levels, including the CEO.[3] One relevant finding is a positive relationship between managerial pay and both the particular job position and the company's size, across all countries. The significant relationship of managerial pay to job position (alternatively, rank in the corporate hierarchy) hints at a form of 'additional incentives' alluded to in my second question.

Lastly, Hall's work summarizes some of his empirical work with Liebman[4] on CEO compensation in the USA, as well as provides an interesting discussion of the value of stock options as an efficient compensation contracting variable. While Hall offers some very interesting insights with respect to the latter; the summary of the findings of his previous work is more relevant to addressing my questions. Let me highlight three of these.

(1) On average, there is a very large pay-for-performance sensitivity exhibited in the compensation contracts of large firms' CEOs;

(2) Over the period 1980–1994, both the level and sensitivity to performance of CEO pay have growth dramatically;

(3) Over the same period, the use of executive stock options has increased significantly.

International pay packages

In light of the evidence above, what can we conclude about the current state of executive remuneration internationally? Are German, Japanese, and American CEOs really subjected to the same pay-for-performance sensitivities as Kaplan suggests? The cheap and apparently obvious answer is: absolutely not. For US CEOs, the cash component of their yearly compensation flows (at least for the

---

[2] These countries comprise a majority of the European Union, including Austria, Belgium, Denmark, Germany, Ireland, Italy, Netherlands, Spain, Switzerland and the UK.

[3] In light of the impending European Union, a reasonable hypothesis is that country-specific effects would have minimal impact in explaining the cross-sectional variation in managerial pay. However, they find significant variations in pay owing to country effects, implying that 'full integration' of the EU is yet to materialize.

[4] See Hall and Liebman (1998).

large firms studied in both Kaplan and Hall) has become smaller and smaller over time. While the absolute levels of cash pay have continued to rise, the reliance upon equity-based pay measures has exploded. In fact, Kaplan (1994) documents an analogous situation in his own comparison of the USA and Japan. He finds that CEO-equivalents in Japan hold roughly one-quarter of the stock held (directly and indirectly through stock options) by American CEOs. If one recalls the work of Jensen and Murphy (1990), all the 'action' in estimates of pay for performance sensitivities stem from movements in the values of CEOs' shares.

So what does this imply for Kaplan's conclusions? For Japan and the USA at least, the inclusion of stock-related pay apparently swings the pendulum back in line with what theory would suggest. That is, firms operating in capital-market based financial systems like that in the USA, rather than in relationship-based financial systems like Japan, must (and apparently do) rely more heavily on explicit contractual solutions such as performance-based pay to mitigate agency problems. One could further argue that the disparity in the use of performance-based pay between the USA and Japan has probably only increased over time in light of Hall's evidence. Therefore, executive incentives provided by compensation contracts do vary significantly across countries, right? Perhaps, but perhaps not.

Alternative incentives given to executives

So what incentives might we be overlooking in these empirical tests of executive compensation? It can be argued that the absolute level of pay offers additional incentives, above and beyond those provided by the structure of the pay. This intuition is garnered from the view that a firm can be thought of as a tournament in which managers compete for the top CEO spot. Economic theory suggests that tournaments provide an efficient means of motivating managers to provide productive labour efforts and make value-maximizing decisions.[5] Essentially, in a tournament, managers compete for a fixed prize. The winner of the prize is chosen on the basis of his/her ranking relative to peers, rather than on absolute performance realizations.

Interestingly, there is strong empirical evidence supporting the efficiency of tournaments. For instance, Ehrenberg and Bognanno (1990) document a positive relationship between the size of the prize and the players' performances turned in for Professional Golf Association (PGA) tournaments. In an experimental setting, Nalbantian and Schotter (1997) document that tournament-based wage schemes generate higher mean outputs than standard (linear) sharing rule schemes that are based on absolute performance. The conclusion appears to be that tournaments work in providing appropriate managerial incentives.

How does this tournament story gel with these papers? To answer this, one

5 See Lazear and Rosen (1981) and Green and Stokey (1983) for the origins of this rich literature.

need only characterize what has happened (and is still happening) to the 'prize' of becoming CEO in the USA. Simply put, the prize has been growing at an exponential rate. According to Hall, the average CEO's compensation has increased by 175% between 1982 and 1994, whereas the average worker's compensation has only increased by 7.2% over the same period. If one thinks of the prize as the relative differential between the top and the bottom of the firm, then the prize to becoming CEO from an average worker's perspective has gone from a 30-times pay increase to a 78-times pay increase.[6] Arguably, a fair return to climbing all the ranks. However, I think it is important to recognize that these enormous prizes for winning an American CEO spot provide incentives not only to managers within the firm, but also CEOs and aspiring CEOs in other firms.

When we couple the incentives provided by both the structure and the level of the pay package, how does this total package vary across countries? The answer depends on the value of winning the CEO prize in other countries. For suggestive evidence, we can look to Crystal (1990) who reports that the ratios of CEO pay to that of the average worker are 21 in Germany, 16 in Japan and 150 in the USA! Coupling this finding with the higher pay for performance sensitivity (including stock) for American CEOs, it seems quite clear that US firms rely much more heavily on pay-based incentives than German or Japanese firms.

The future of executive incentives

Given the arguments above, could Kaplan's claim possibly be right? Actually, I believe the answer is yes for two reasons. First, notice that thus far I have only discussed the pecuniary benefits to winning a CEO post. The prize to winning the corporate tournament may in fact be dominated by the non-pecuniary benefits of control, which stem from increased power and prestige. For obvious reasons, estimating the value of these is quite difficult. However, it can be argued that the cultures of Germany and Japan may offer greater private benefits of control to their executives than in the USA. Thus, with the inclusion of these benefits as part of the CEO-prize, America's lead over the other countries in terms of providing total managerial incentives is probably diminished.

The second reason supporting Kaplan's claim relates to the manner in which corporations now operate in the market for executive talent. The dynamics of this market have changed dramatically in the last 10 years, both in the USA and globally. In fact, I would argue that what has given rise to this ever-increasing CEO-prize is the increased mobility of executive talent. Firms no longer restrict themselves to fill their helms with insiders. Many of the recent CEO appointments have been across industries. In discussing just such a

---

6 Obviously, the natural progression through the managerial ranks would include a greater number of steps than one!

change, Helyar and Lublin (1998) in the *Wall Street Journal Europe (WSJE)*, noted that a "banker-turned-utility executive runs Delta Air Lines [and] a former finance professor and cereal executive runs Times Mirror Co". Simply put, firms are now seeking out the best in managerial talent, and not necessarily searching for the best man in the industry. Why does this matter? These top executives such as George Fisher and Albert Dunlap carry with them a very high reservation wage owing to their reputations. These higher reservation wages then map into spectacular compensation packages designed to lure them to any given firm.[7]

Apparently, this phenomenon of the 'winners' receiving a larger prize in recent years reaches far beyond corporate America. Frank and Cook (1995), in their book entitled *The Winner-Takes-All Society*, claim the following: "These high stakes have created a new class of unknown celebrities: those pivotal players who spell the difference between corporate success and failure. Because their performance is crucial, and because modern information technology has helped build consensus about who they are, rival organizations must compete furiously to hire and retain them.

The widening gap is apparently not new ... Alfred Marshall wrote over a century ago, '... the relative fall in the incomes to be earned by those of moderate ability, however carefully trained, is accentuated by the rise in those that are obtained by many men of extraordinary ability'."

What does this imply about the future of cross-country variations in managerial incentives? It suggests that if European and Japanese corporations begin hiring more executive 'superstars' to run their firms, an explosion of international CEO pay will unfold for the tournament winners. Is this happening? According to the same *WSJE* report, CEOs now "hopscotch around the corporate world, over national borders, and across all industry boundaries. [For example,] in France, an elite cadre of leaders with the right educational and social pedigrees often skip from industry to industry." Analogous examples of small groups of top executives rising to the top in terms of reputation were offered for Germany, the Netherlands and Sweden. Therefore, let me conclude with the prediction that if the trend in executive mobility continues, then these international superstars will soon command compensation packages that rival their American counterparts. This could certainly bring Kaplan's claim of 'near-equal' global incentive structures to fruition quite quickly.

References

Crystal, G. (1991). *In Search of Excess: The Overcompensation of American Executives*, W.W. Norton, New York.

[7] Interestingly, a CEO's reputation is also positively related to pay for performance sensitivity. Milbourn (1997) shows theoretically that it is optimal for shareholders to offer highly performance-sensitive contracts to those CEOs with the highest reputations. This prediction is supported by the data in his paper.

Ehrenberg, R.G. and M.L. Bognanno (1990). Do tournaments have incentive effects? *Journal of Political Economy*, **98**, 1307–1324.

Frank, R.H. and P.J. Cook (1995). *The Winner-Take-All Society.* The Free Press, New York.

Green, J.R. and N.L. Stokey (1983). A comparison of tournaments and contracts. *Journal of Political Economy*, 91–3, 349–364.

Hall, B. and J. Liebman (1998). Are CEOs really paid like bureaucrats?, *Quarterly Journal of Economics*, forthcoming.

Helyar, J. and J. Lublin (1998). The portable CEO. *Wall Street Journal Europe*, January 22, p. A1.

Jensen, M. and K.J. Murphy (1990). Performance pay and top-management incentives. *Journal of Political Economy,* **98**, 225–262.

Kaplan, S.N. (1994). Top executive rewards and firm performance: a comparison of Japan and the United States. *Journal of Political Economy*, **102**, 510–546.

Lazear, E.P. and S. Rosen (1981). Rank-order tournaments as optimum labor contracts. *Journal of Political Economy,* **89**, 841–864.

Milbourn, T.T. (1997). The Executive Compensation Puzzle: Theory and Evidence. London Business School, IFA Working Paper no. 235–1996.

Nalbantian, H.R. and A. Schotter (1997). Productivity under group incentives: an experimental study, *American Economic Review,* **87**, 314–341.

PART TWO

KEVIN F. HALLOCK
University of Illinois at Urbana-Champaign

5. Dual agency: corporate boards with reciprocally interlocking relationships

INTRODUCTION

This paper studies reciprocal interlocks of boards of directors of large firms where an employee of firm A sits on firm B's board and at the same time an employee of firm B sits on firm A's board. The study of Boards of Directors by those in economics and finance is not new. In fact, Dooley (1969) writes of interlocking directorates, but his definition is different in that he presents evidence of interlock where "at least one director ... sat on the board of at least one other of the largest companies". Books by Mizruchi (1982) and Pennings (1980) as well as many articles, for example Bearden and Mintz (1985), Bunting and Barbour (1971) and Mintz and Schwartz (1981) discuss interlocking boards in much more detail from a sociological perspective. Mizruchi and Stearns (1988) study the longitudinal formation of interlocking directorates using a small sample of firms.

This paper uses data from the early 1990s to explore reciprocal interlocks and the effects they have on firms. There are several goals, including documenting the frequency of interlocks and the characteristics of boards that interlock, exploring several different definitions of reciprocal interlock, examining whether interlocks are symptomatic of agency problems, and whether interlocks have an effect on managerial pay.[1]

INTERLOCK TYPES AND SAMPLE CHARACTERISTICS

The sample frame used in the paper is firms listed in the *Forbes* magazine 500s list which is a list of the 500 largest firms in each of four categories, sales, profits, assets, and market value, in 1992; 773 unique firms made the list in that year. I collected detailed information on the boards of directors for each of the firms in the sample from annual and proxy reports. Table 1 is an example of the kind of data collected for one of the firms, Merck & Company. For each director I collected the name, occupation, principal employer, and whether the person was retired from his or her main job. The entire data set includes 9,804

[1] Hallock (1997) provides a detailed examination of the link between managerial pay and board interlocks.

J. Carpenter and D. Yermack (eds.), Executive Compensation and Shareholder Value, 55–75.

Table 1. Example of Director Data for Merck & Company, 1992[a]

Firm	*Last*	*First*	*Middle*	*Occupation*	*Employer*	*Retired*
Merck	Atwater	H	Brewster	CH-CEO	General Mills	0
Merck	Birkin	Derek		CH	RTZ	0
Merck	Bossidy	Lawrence	A	CH-CEO	Allied Signal	0
Merck	Bowen	William	G	PR	Andrew W Mellon	0
Merck	Davis	Carolyne	K	Consultant	Self	0
Merck	Elam	Lloyd	C	Professor	Meharry Medical	0
Merck	Exley	Charles	E	CH-CEO	NCR	1
Merck	Horan	John	J	CH-CEO	Merck	1
Merck	Kelley	William	N	CEO	University of Pennsylvania Medical Center	0
Merck	Markham	Richard	J	PR-COO	Merck	0
Merck	Merck	Albert	W	Trustee	Merck Family Trusts	0
Merck	Mettler	Ruben	F	CH-CEO	TRW	1
Merck	Ross	Richard	S	Dean	Johns Hopkins University	1
Merck	Vagelos	P	Roy	CH-CEO	Merck	0
Merck	Weatherstone	Dennis		CH	JP Morgan & Company	0

[a]For each director and for all firms, the data include the last name, the first name, the middle name, the principal occupation, the principal employer, and whether or not the individual is retired from his or her main occupation. Retired = 1 if the individual is retired from his or her main occupation, 0 otherwise. The entire director data set includes 772 other tables that are set up precisely like this one.

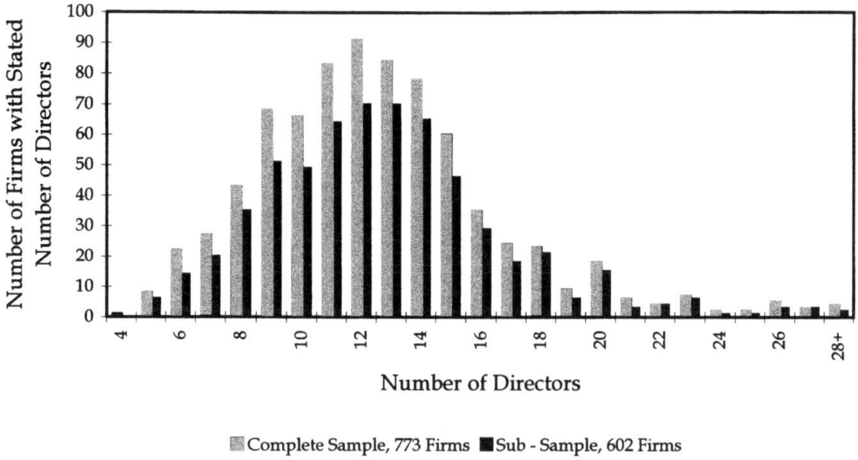

Figure 1. Distribution of number of directors per firm

director seats held by 7,519 individuals.[2] Figure 1 shows the distribution of the number of directors per board. The average is 13 and it is clear from the figure that most boards in this sample have between 9 and 15 members.

It was important to collect information on all firms, as if one of the sample firms was excluded then remaining firms may actually look not interlocked when, in fact, they were. In some cases, therefore, I needed to supplement the data with additional information from other sources such as *The Million Dollar Directory, Standard & Poor's Register of Corporations, Directors, and Executives, The Directory of Corporate Affiliations, Who's Who in Finance and Industry,* Lexis-Nexis, and Laser Disclosure.

The first interlock type is what I call current-CEO interlock. Firms A and B are current-CEO interlocked if the current CEO from firm A is a member of firm B's board and the current CEO from firm B is a member of firm A's board. Figure 2 is a histogram of the fraction interlocked by interlock type. There are two bars for each type of interlock (others explained below), representing the entire sample of 773 firms, and the subsample ($n = 602$) which contains all additional data used elsewhere in the paper for each firm. About 8% of the firms are current-CEO interlocked.

Second, firms A and B are current-employee interlocked if any current employee of firm A (including the CEO) serves as a director of firm B and if any current employee of firm B (including the CEO) serves as a director of firm A. About 12% of firms are current-employee interlocked.

The third and fourth measures of interlocking only consider individuals who have retired from their main jobs. Retired individuals are not as likely to have

[2] There are fewer individuals than seats as some individuals serve on more than one board.

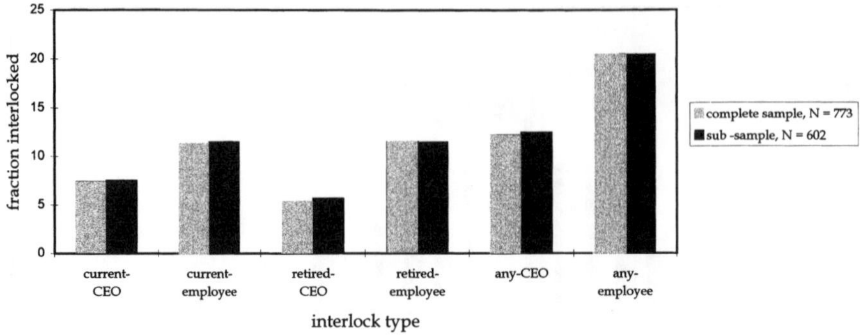

Figure 2. Fraction interlocked by interlock type

such direct input in a reciprocal arrangement. However, since they were employees of the firms in question they may have participated in a stronger form of interlock prior to becoming retired. Retired-CEO interlock occurs between firms A and B when a retired CEO of firm A serves as a director of firm B and a retired CEO of firm B serves as a director of firm A. Firms A and B are retired-employee interlocked when any retired employee (including retired CEOs) of firm A serves as a director of firm B and any retired employee (including retired CEOs) of firm B serves as a director of firm A. The fraction interlocked for these two groups are not significantly different using these measures relative to those interlocked via current employees.

The fifth measure of interlock is any-CEO interlock. Firms A and B are any-CEO interlocked when a current or retired CEO of firm A serves as a director of firm B and a current or retired CEO of firm B serves as a director of firm A. Of course each firm that is current-CEO interlocked or that is retired-CEO interlocked is also any-CEO interlocked, but some firms that are neither current-CEO interlocked nor retired-CEO interlocked may be any-CEO interlocked. This occurs, for example, when the current CEO of firm A sits on firm B's board and a retired CEO of firm B sits on firm A's board. Any-CEO interlock occurs in about 12% of firms.[3]

Any-employee interlock is the sixth and most comprehensive interlock measure. Two firms are any-employee interlocked if any current or retired employee of firm A serves as a director of firm B and vice versa. Any firm that is current-employee interlocked or that is retired-employee interlocked must be any-employee interlocked but additional firms can be also. This occurs, for example, when the current Vice President of firm A serves on firm B's board and the retired Treasurer of firm B serves on firm A's board. Roughly 20% of firms are any-employee interlocked.

---

[3] The sum of the fraction of firms current-CEO interlocked and retired-CEO interlocked can be greater than the fraction any-CEO interlocked since some firms can be simultaneously current-CEO interlocked and retired-CEO interlocked.

Some of the characteristics of the boards are listed in Table 2. The average number of directors per firm is 12.71, the average fraction of inside directors is 0.25, and the average proportion of directors on a given board who are principally employed by one of the other large firms is 0.44. The table also computes averages for these variables for the any-employee interlocked and non any-employee interlocked groups separately.

Interlocked boards have, on average, more directors, fewer insiders, and are more likely to have directors from one of the other sample firms. Table 2 also lists the average market value of equity (collected from Compustat) and the average stock return (collected from CRSP). Interlocked firms are much larger (in terms of market value of equity) than non-interlocked firms although the returns are not significantly different. Finally, Table 2 lists the 12 primary occupations for board members and the average fraction for each per board.

Table 2. Summary Statistics for Boards and Firms

	All	*Non any-employee interlocked*	*Any-employee interlocked*
Number of directors	12.71[b] (0.16)	12.32 (0.19)	14.24 (0.15)
Proportion insiders	0.25[b] (.01)	0.26 (0.01)	0.23 (0.01)
Proportion of directors employed by one of original sample firms	0.44[b] (0.01)	0.41 (0.01)	0.54 (0.01)
Market value of equity ($millions)	4,843[b] (336)	3,783 (324)	8,973 (975)
Stock return[a] in year t-1	0.48 (0.03)	0.49 (0.03)	0.44 (0.04)
Proportion of directors per firm who list primary occupation as			
CEO	0.32[b] (0.01)	0.29 (0.01)	0.41 (0.01)
Chairman	0.13 (0.004)	0.13 (0.01)	0.14 (0.01)
President	0.16[b] (0.004)	0.16 (0.01)	0.14 (0.01)
Vice chairman	0.05 (0.003)	0.05 (0.003)	0.06 (0.01)
Vice president	0.10[b] (0.01)	0.11 (0.005)	0.08 (0.01)
Professor	0.04[d] (0.003)	0.03 (0.003)	0.04 (0.004)
Attorney	0.02[c] (0.002)	0.02 (0.002)	0.01 (0.003)
Doctor	0.003 (0.0001)	0.003 (0.001)	0.001 (0.001)
Government official	0.01[c] (0.001)	0.007 (0.001)	0.013 (0.002)
Consultant	0.02[d] (0.002)	0.024 (0.002)	0.016 (0.003)
Businessman	0.09[b] (0.004)	0.09 (0.01)	0.07 (0.01)
Other occupation	0.07[b] (0.004)	0.08 (0.01)	0.03 (0.004)
n	602	479	123

[a]Annual stock return from CRSP in 1991. All other data from 1992. [b,c,d]Mean differences between last two columns at 0.01, 0.05, and 0.10 levels. Standard errors are in parentheses.

ARE INTERLOCKS DUE TO AGENCY PROBLEMS?

Before I examine any effects of interlock on firms, it is important to try to study what interlocks really mean. Are interlocks cronyism? Are interlocks representative of customer/supplier, banking, or other business relationships among firms? Are interlocks simply representative of firm ownership? Do interlocked firms have lower accounting or stock market returns than non-interlocked firms? Do interlocks occur any more frequently than would be expected by random chance?

Are interlocks just random assignment?

What fraction of firms would be interlocked if directors were randomly assigned to board positions? We should not think *a priori* that this fraction is zero. In this section I focus on the broadest measure of interlock, any-employee interlock. To test whether the fraction any-employee interlocked is simply an artifact of random assignment, I simulate what the true fraction interlocked would be under a set of assumptions. First I assume that the actual board sizes and populations of directors are exogenous. That is, the directors who are currently in my sample are the entire population of potential directors. I further assume that for each of the 999 iterations of randomly assigning directors, each director position will be reassigned a spot in the sample. Finally, I assume that interlocks are allowed within an industry[4] as well as across industries.

The results of the simulations are shown in Table 3. The first row describes the data from the complete sample of 773 firms. In those firms there are 9,804 director seats filled by 7,519 individual directors. The actual fraction any-employee interlocked is 20%, which is much larger than the 4.4% we would find if these directors were assigned to positions randomly. The second row (top 500 sales) repeats the analysis for the largest 500 firms by sales. In this subsample, a larger fraction of the firms are interlocked, 24%. Although there are fewer firms in this sample with which to interlock, larger firms are much more likely to interlock. Therefore the fraction interlocked in this smaller sample is larger. The simulated fraction in this subsample is also larger, at 8%, but still substantially smaller than the actual fraction. The rest of the top panel in Table 3 shows the simulated and actual fraction interlocked for various subsamples of the director data. As the sample size is decreased, both the true and simulated fraction interlocked tend to increase but the true fraction interlocked remains substantially larger than the simulated fraction.

In light of a comment by Jensen and Murphy (1990) that "disclosure of top-management compensation can help guard against 'looting' by management (in collusion with 'captive' boards of directors)" we might guess that the true fraction interlocked might be smaller today than was the case in an earlier

[4] Technically employees of one firm cannot serve as directors for another firm in the same industry according to the Clayton Act of 1914. However, even though there have been potential violations of the act, it is very rarely enforced (see Dooley, 1969).

Table 3. Actual and simulated fraction of interlocking directorships using data from two years[a]

Firms	*Seats*	*Directors*	*Simulated fraction any-employee-interlocked*	*Actual fraction any-employee-interlocked*
Data from 1992				
Top 773	9,804	7,519	0.0435 (0.0003)	0.2040 (0.0146)
Top 500 (sales)	6,441	4,773	0.0768 (0.0005)	0.2400 (0.0191)
Top 400 (sales)	5,285	3,912	0.0957 (0.0006)	0.2650 (0.0221)
Top 300 (sales)	4,048	3,003	0.1178 (0.0008)	0.2933 (0.0263)
Top 252 (sales)	3,469	2,593	0.1386 (0.0009)	0.2857 (0.0285)
Data from 1976				
Top 252 (sales)	3,976	3,108	0.1431 (0.0009)	0.0754 (0.0167)

[a]The first panel uses the data collected from 1992 and the second panel uses data from 1976. In Panel A Top 773 represents the entire director sample from 1992. This is all 773 of the *Forbes 500s* firms. Seats are the actual number of board director positions. For all 773 firms there were 9804 seats. However, since some directors serve on more than one board there were only 7519 unique directors in the top 773 firms. To perform the simulations, I assume that (1) directors who are currently in my sample are the entire sample of potential directors, (2) each director position has probability one of being randomly reassigned a spot in the sample, and (3) interlocks are allowed within industry. 999 iterations are performed for each sample. The actual fraction of any-employee interlocked firms is reported in the last column. Interlocking appears to happen much more frequently than if directors were randomly assigned to boards. Each row in the top panel represents a different sample from the data. The bottom panel reports results using the 252 largest firms in terms of sales in 1976. This is the size of the sample obtained from Bearden and Mintz (1985). (Standard errors are reported in parentheses).

period, as disclosure has become more common and SEC rules more strict. Surprisingly, this is not the case. Although the simulated fraction (if directors are assigned randomly) is very similar in 1992 (penultimate row in Table 3) and 1976 (last row in Table 3; 13.9 vs. 14.3%), the actual fraction is much larger in 1992 relative to 1976 (28.6 vs. 7.5%).[5] This could be the result of measurement error in the collection of the data for 1976 but could also be due to the increased numbers of joint venture and other business relationship or customer supplier relationships among firms over the time period.

Anti-takeover amendments, poison pills and golden parachutes

To answer additional questions about agency costs I tried to study whether the firms had (1) anti-takeover amendments, (2) golden parachutes or (3) poison pills by exploring the annual reports, proxy statements, 10Qs, and 10Ks for a large subset (602) of the original 773 firms in a very simple way.[6] A positive

[5] I thank Beth Mintz and James Bearden for access to their director data set from 1976.

association between interlock and these phenomena might imply agency conflicts. For a given firm, I searched using a computer through the reports for the words, anti-takeover, golden parachute, and poison pill. If one of these words was detected, I read the text more carefully and a determined whether these phenomena actually existed in these firms.

Table 4 shows that although the fraction of any-employee interlocked firms that have poison pills and anti-takeover amendments is higher than the fraction for non-interlocked firms, the difference is not statistically significant. However, the fraction of any employee interlocked firms that have golden parachutes is lower than the fraction of non-interlocked firms (the results are the same for the five other measures of interlock). Even if we were willing to assume that poison pills, anti-takeover amendments or golden parachutes were symptomatic of agency conflicts (and that this is a good method for finding them), the data do not provide strong evidence that interlocked firms are more likely to have them.

Table 4. Fraction of any-employee interlocked firms and non any-employee interlocked firms with poison pills, anti-takeover amendments, and golden parachutes[a]

	Non any-employee interlocked firms (n=479)	*Any-employee interlocked firms (n=123)*
Poison pill	3.97% (0.89)	5.69% (2.10)
Anti-takeover amendment	7.93% (1.24)	9.76% (2.69)
Golden parachute	3.34% (0.82)	0.81% (0.81)

[a]Two firms are any-employee interlocked if any current or retired employee of firm A is a director of firm B and vice versa. For these 602 firms a determination was made about whether the firms have poison pills, anti-takeover amendments, or golden parachutes by reviewing annuals reports, proxy statements, 10Ks and 10Qs for each firm. (Standard errors are reported in parentheses).

Customer/supplier, banking and other business relationships

It may also be the case that interlocks simply reflect other kinds of business relationships such as customer/supplier, banking, or other business relationships and that they are not, therefore, cronyism at all. For each interlocked firm I studied annual reports, proxy statements, 10Ks and 10Qs to study why these firms were interlocked. For each firm I again searched with a computer through the reports for the name of the firm to which it was interlocked. When the computer found the name of the other firm in these reports a determination was made as to whether the firms had a customer/supplier, banking, other business relationship, or a relationship not explained by one of the other three

[6] Some firms were excluded since all reports could not be located.

Table 5. Fraction of any-employee and any-CEO interlocked firms with customer/supplier, banking, or other business relationships[a]

	Any-employee interlock (n = 123)	*Any-CEO interlock (n = 75)*
Customer/supplier relationship	13.01% (3.05)	10.67% (3.59)
Banking relationship	6.50% (2.23)	13.33% (2.28)
Other business relationship	14.63% (3.20)	13.33% (3.95)

[a]Two firms are any-CEO interlocked if a current or retired CEO of firm A serves as a director of firm B and a current or retired CEO of firm B is a director of firm A. Two firms are any-employee interlocked if any current or retired employee of firm A is a director of firm B and vice versa. I studied whether the firms have customer/supplier, banking, or other business relationships by going back to annual reports, proxy statements, 10Ks and 10Qs for each interlocked firm. For example, if firm A was interlocked with firm B, a computer searched through each of firm A's reports looking for reference to firm B. When a reference was found, a determination was made about whether these relationships were customer/supplier, banking, other business relationships, or none of the others. (Standard errors are reported in parentheses)

categories. Table 5 shows the fraction of interlocked firms whose interlocks are relationship-based. For example, two firms that participate in a joint venture are considered to have a business relationship. The first column is the fraction of any-employee interlocked firms with these relationships. The second column is the fraction of any-CEO interlocked firms with these relationships.

Although this clearly does not account for all interlocks which are due to business relationships, a strong case can be made that cronyism is less likely to be a problem in the firms with these kinds of arrangements. A number of firms seem to be interlocked for business reasons. For example, of any-employee interlocked firms, 13% had identifiable customer/supplier relationships, and 15% had other business relationships. Firms that have at least one customer/supplier, banking, or other business relationship make up 26% of the any-employee interlocked firms and 22% of the any-CEO interlocked firms (clearly some of the firms have more than one of these relationships at once). This section seems to lend some evidence against the notion that interlock is just cronyism; however, a large fraction of interlocks remain unexplained by business relationships. Part of the analysis below on managerial compensation (Table 8) separates firms into all interlocked firms and those who are interlocked for reasons unexplained by customer/supplier, banking, or other business relationships. Although one cannot be certain, it is possible that the remaining firms are more likely to have agency costs than the former.

CEO and officer and director ownership

I also analysed whether interlock might just mean ownership of the firm. If it were the case that firms currently headed by founders or firms whose CEO owned larger share holdings (either in terms of proportion of stock owned or total value of shares held) or firms whose officers and directors had larger ownership interests, were systematically more likely to be interlocked, then the interlock variable may mean something other than cronyism and something more like ownership over the firm. If the owner and manager are the same, there is no agency conflict. To help study this I have collected the percent of stock in the firm owned by the chief executive and the fraction owned by officers and directors from *Forbes*. These are included as measures of ownership structure. It may be the case that if a CEO owns more of the stock of the firm for which he is employed, his interests are more in line with those of the shareholders than otherwise.

I ran probit models where the dependent variable was any-employee interlock (not reported in the tables). Explanatory variables included CEO, officer, and director share ownership, an indicator variable for whether the CEO is a founder, firm equity value, and stock market return. Various tests suggest that CEOs with more control in terms of ownership are not more likely to be interlocked.

Performance

Do interlocked firms have lower performance than other firms? Lower profits or returns for interlocked firms might be suggestive of agency conflicts. Although interlocked firms have a lower point estimate of returns, the effects are insignificant for each measure of return: stock return (see Table 2), return on assets, and return on equity.

To summarize, there is some reason to believe that interlock is due to agency conflicts. First, simulation estimates suggest that interlocking happens far more often than can be explained by random chance. Second, although up to 26% of interlocks can be explained by customer/supplier, banking, or other business relationships, a large proportion of interlocking cannot be. Third, more interlocked firms adopt poison pills and anti-takeover amendments than non-interlocked firms (although the difference is not statistically significant). Fourth, interlocked firms tend to have lower returns (although insignificantly so) than non-interlocked firms. Finally, interlock does not seem to be correlated with firm ownership. Taken together, these facts suggest that interlock could be due to agency problems in corporate governance.

DUAL AGENCY MODEL AND MANAGERIAL PAY

Theories of managerial compensation and background

In the extensive literature on executive compensation, two theories, pay for productivity (Murphy, 1985) and tournaments (Lazear and Rosen, 1981), have received the most attention. However, neither of these directly examines the role of the body which sets executive pay – the board of directors. The pay for productivity literature is characterized in a paper by Murphy (1985). The basic building block of most pay for productivity models, especially in regard to CEO pay, is the principal-agent relationship. The principal (the shareholders or owners of the firm) cannot perfectly observe the actions of the agent (the CEO). In order to motivate an executive, the employer can use a measure of the CEO's performance, such as the stock market return, paying him more if the measure is high and less if it is low.

The typical approach in testing pay for productivity models is to regress the natural logarithm of compensation on a set of CEO and firm characteristics, often taken from panel data. Standard firm control variables include firm size in terms of stock market value or sales. The important explanatory variable in the productivity model is firm performance, measured for example, by the stock market return of the firm.[7] If a positive relationship exists between stock market return and CEO pay, then it is argued the CEOs are doing well for the firm.

Finally, the modern tournament literature was started by Lazear and Rosen (1981). The basis of this literature is the idea that firm compensation should be interpreted as a prize for superior job performance. The ultimate prize in a given firm is the job of CEO, whose salary is typically the highest in the firm. This is not because he is worth that much, but rather that this higher salary offers incentives to the others in the firm to work harder in competition for the prize. If a firm offers a wage that is, say, twice the CEO's marginal product, this still may be efficient for the employer since one should take into consideration not only the marginal product of the CEO but also the marginal products of the other managers in the firm who might have a chance of one day becoming CEO.[8]

Dual agency

Existing models describe managerial compensation quite well but they ignore an important ingredient of the make-up of compensation for CEOs. The composition of the Board of Directors, which ultimately votes on a given CEO's compensation, may yield additional information in helping to describe salaries of CEOs.[9]

Many of the CEOs of large firms are directors of other large firms. If a CEO

---

7 Two of the most influential papers in this literature are Murphy (1985) and Jensen and Murphy (1990). Other papers include Baker *et al.* (1988), Bizjak *et al.* (1993), Ciscel (1974), Ciscel and Carroll (1980), Coughlan and Schmidt (1985), DiNardo *et al.* (1997), Ehrenberg and Milkovich (1987), Gibbons and Murphy (1990), Hallock (1997, 1998), Hallock and Oyer (1997), Lambert and Larker (1988), Lewellen and Huntsman (1970), Masson (1971), Murphy (1986), Roberts (1956) and Sloan (1993). Hall and Liebman (1997) provide an interesting new look at these issues.

8 Related work includes Baker *et al.* (1993), Leonard (1990) and O'Reilly *et al.* (1988).

9 If it were true that directors acted exactly in the interests of shareholders, then we would not have to explicitly account for board structure.

of firm 1 is on the Board of Directors of firm 2 and if a CEO of firm 2 is on the Board of Directors of firm 1, then the CEOs may have unusual opportunities to increase each other's salaries. I refer to this situation (above) as current-CEO interlock. Additionally, many non-CEO employees of firms in the sample serve as directors of other firms in the sample. These non-CEO employees are important for two reasons. The first is that they may someday become CEOs themselves. Second, CEO compensation appears to be linked with the compensation of other top managers (see Arreglado, 1993).

The basic hypothesis that reciprocal interlock can lead to higher salaries for both CEOs can be formalized by thinking of a simple model in which each board has only one director. In the absence of interlock, the CEO of firm 1 is an agent for the owners of the firm represented by the board. Standard principal-agent models (e.g., Fama, 1980; Gibbons and Murphy, 1992; Holmstrom, 1979; Jensen and Meckling, 1976) suggest that the board will try to design a compensation package to maximize the value of the firm, after paying the CEO. Suppose now that CEO1 is the director of firm 2 and CEO2 is the director of firm 1. Then these two CEOs could be thought of as a pair of agents who ideally have to negotiate with the collective set of owners of firm 1 and firm 2. If the compensation of CEO1 is left in the hands of CEO2 and vice versa, it is difficult to imagine that their salaries will be set at the optimal levels from the perspective of the firms. Thus, the name dual agency. Interlocking directorates can potentially threaten the board's ability to objectively set salaries on behalf of the firm's owners. Bowen (1994) suggests, for example, that "[in] selecting board members, care should be taken to avoid incestuous relationships and to preserve a certain amount of distance between board members and the CEO". It remains an empirical issue whether reciprocally interlocking directorates pose any serious problems.

There are other board member to CEO relationships which are not explored here. Consultants and representatives of law firms often sit on boards of directors. It might be difficult for these types of directors to deny large pay increases to CEOs given that the CEO may single-handedly have full authority to relieve them (or their firms) from their services.

MANAGERIAL COMPENSATION – DO INTERLOCKS MATTER?

"The very high salaries we observe in many American corporations may not be optimal prizes, but simply a way in which corporate directors distribute rents to their friends in the executive suite. This suspicion is reinforced by the frequency with which the CEOs of one corporation serve as directors of another." – Rees (1992)

Background

An earlier study by Williamson (1963) suggests a relationship between the compensation of the top executive and other variables, including 'composition of the board'. Controlling for administrative, general, and selling expenses (i.e., staff) of the firm, the concentration ratio in the industry, and the height of barriers to entry in the firm's industry, he finds that the proportion of the board represented by inside managers (those who are principally employed by the firm for which they serve as director) has an insignificantly positive effect on CEO compensation.[10]

Work by Weisbach (1988) and Hermalin and Weisbach (1988) also looks at inside vs. outside directors in relation to CEO turnover, which can be thought of as a crude measure of compensation.[11] Weisbach concludes "There is a stronger association between prior performance and the probability of resignation for companies with outsider-dominated boards than for companies with insider-dominated boards". Hermalin and Weisbach write that "When their CEO nears retirement, firms tend to add inside directors (and) just after a CEO change, inside directors with short tenures appear more likely to leave the board". They also found that inside directors are more likely to leave a board after a firm performs poorly and when a firm exits a market, and outside directors are more likely to join.[12]

A group of authors has begun studying the differences among three theories: 'social comparison', economic and psychological. O'Reilly *et al.* (1988), using a sample of 105 firms, found a "strong association between CEO compensation and the compensation of outside members of the board of directors", even when controlling for return on assets, sales, and assets. Belliveau *et al.* (1996) used a sample of 61 firms and concluded that "social similarity and status differences significantly increase CEO compensation after controlling for variables representing economic, social comparison, and other social influence explanations for CEO compensation". Main *et al.* (1995) also studied whether the CEO's social influence over the board can yield higher CEO pay. They found, for example, that CEOs appointed before the chairs of their compensation committees received 11% more pay than CEOs appointed after their compensation committee chairs. Finally, Newman and Wright (1995) found, in a sample of 161 firms, that CEOs who have at least one insider on their compensation committees have higher compensation.

---

10 Other authors such as Mayers and Smith (1992) also consider the relative fraction of insiders to outsiders (also see Rediker and Seth, 1995).

11 Dismissal is a form of very low compensation.

12 Kaplan and Minton (1994) investigated the appointments of outside directors to boards in Japan and the USA. They found that turnover of Japanese executives was higher in the years where outside directors employed by banks or other nonfinancial companies are added to boards. They conclude that "banks and corporate shareholders play an important monitoring and disciplinary role in Japan." Kaplan (1994) found that in Germany, where there are both supervisory and management boards, board turnover increases with poor stock performance. Yermack (1996) provides an interesting examination and shows an "inverse association between board size and firm value."

Returns to interlock

This section is aimed at three issues. First, do CEOs who lead interlocked firms earn more? Second, does the 'return' to interlock vary by definition of interlock (from, for example, considering current CEOs vs. retired CEOs)? Third, does redefining those interlocked firms that have documented customer/supplier, banking, or other business relationships as not interlocked affect the return to interlock?

The 1992 data on CEO compensation and characteristics are from *Forbes* magazine's annual compensation survey. There are three primary measures of pay: (1) salary plus bonus, (2) salary plus bonus plus other (which includes such items as the value of contributions to savings plans and memberships to clubs) and (3) total compensation (which is the sum of (2) plus exercised options).[13] *Forbes* also reports information on the CEO's age, seniority as CEO and seniority with the firm, as well as other variables.

Table 6 displays means of the variables on CEOs for any-employee and non any-employee interlocked firms separately. The CEOs earned between $1.1 and $2.6 million depending on how pay was measured. The average age of the CEOs was 57, the average seniority in the firm was 24 years and the average seniority as CEO was 9 years. Interlocked CEOs earned more, were older, and had been CEO for fewer years than CEOs who were not interlocked.

Table 7 begins to answer the first of the three questions posed at the beginning of this section.[14] The last three columns in Table 7 show raw wage differentials for the three measures of pay. For example, current-CEO interlocked firms pay their CEOs an average of 32.63% more than non-current-CEO interlocked firms. For the first two measures of pay, it is clear from the tables that CEOs heading interlocked firms earn substantially more than CEOs who are not. This is not universally true, however, for the third measure of pay (total compensation), but as I stated earlier, this is an unusual way to measure pay. However, as we have seen in Table 2, interlocked firms have several easily observed characteristics (for example market value of equity is much higher in interlocked firms) that are much different from non-interlocked firms. Perhaps interlock picks up these other variables.

Table 8 presents coefficients on interlock indicator variables from least squares regressions of compensation on interlock and control variables such as the CEO's age and its square, the CEO's seniority in the firm and its square, the CEO's seniority as CEO and its square, the ln(firm market value of equity), lagged stock return, the number of directors and 20 industry indicator variables. The six columns have two columns each for ln(salary plus bonus),

---

[13] Note that this includes the value of options when exercised, not when granted, so this variable clearly has noise associated with it. A better variable would be (2) plus the current value of options granted in a given year. Recent rule changes by the SEC have made collecting the value of options granted in a given year much easier.

[14] See Hallock (1997) for additional explanation of the interlock effect on executive compensation..

Table 6. Summary Statistics For CEOs[a]

	All	*Non-any-employee interlocked*	*Any-employee interlocked*
CEO's age (years)	56.98[b] (0.27)	56.75 (0.32)	57.88 (0.43)
CEO's firm seniority (years)	23.72[b] (0.49)	22.62 (0.56)	28.02 (0.87)
CEO's seniority as CEO (years)	8.52[b] (0.31)	8.87 (0.36)	7.17 (0.28)
CEO's salary plus bonus ($millions)	1.10[b] (0.04)	1.05 (0.05)	1.27 (0.06)
CEO's salary + bonus + other ($millions)	1.35[b] (0.05)	1.28 (0.06)	1.64 (0.08)
CEO's total compensation ($millons)	2.57 (0.23)	2.45 (0.23)	3.05 (0.63)
n	602	479	123

[a]Summary statistics are presented for all, for non any-employee interlocked firms, and for any-employee interlocked firms. Two firms are any-employee interlocked if any current or retired employee (including CEOs) of firm A serves as a director of firm B and if any current or retired employee (including CEOs) of firm B serves as a director of firm A. The measures of compensation are (salary plus bonus), (salary plus bonus plus other compensation), and (total compensation). Other compensation includes such items as insurance policies, restricted shares that vested during the year, savings plan contributions, memberships to clubs, etc. Total compensation is the sum of salary plus bonus plus other compensation plus exercised options. These compensation data are from Forbes magazine and are for 1992.
[b]Mean differences between the last two columns at 0.01 level of significance. Standard deviations are in parentheses.

ln(salary plus bonus plus other), and ln(total compensation) as the dependent variable, respectively. The rows represent which interlock type is controlled for. Only the return to interlock coefficients and their standard errors are displayed in Table 8. Each set of two numbers in the table represents a different regression.

Columns 1, 3, and 5 use the six standard interlocking definitions defined above. The returns to interlock seem to vary somewhat by measure of compensation. The returns to interlock using ln(salary plus bonus), and ln(salary plus bonus plus other) are always positive and in one case large and statistically significant. The returns to interlock using ln(total compensation) are never significant and sometimes even negative. This is not particularly surprising given the discussion above that this is a poor measure of compensation. Although the measures vary somewhat, it is puzzling that the return to current-CEO interlock is smaller than the return to current employee interlock and that the retired interlock return measures are typically the same or only slightly smaller than the current ones. Clearly, controlling for the additional covariates has a significant effect on the large positive returns to interlock implied by Table 7.

Columns 2, 4, and 6 of Table 8 help to answer the third question: 'does redefining those interlocked firms that have documented customer/supplier,

Table 7. Interlocked vs non-interlocked percentage compensation differentials for various measures of interlocking and three measures of compensation[a]

		((Interlocked pay) – (Non-interlocked pay)) / (Non-interlocked pay)		
Interlock type	*Fraction interlocked*	*Salary plus bonus*	*Salary plus bonus plus other*	*Total compensation*
1. Current-CEO	7.48	32.63[c]	29.29[c]	63.79[d]
2. Current-employee	11.46	27.78[c]	20.21[b]	36.22
3. Retired-CEO	5.65	20.36	18.42	–15.76
4. Retired-employee	11.46	19.83[d]	25.52[c]	17.42
5. Any-CEO	12.45	29.79[c]	26.88[c]	34.27
6. Any-employee	20.43	21.05[c]	28.20[b]	24.65

[a]The first measure of interlock is 1. current-CEO interlock. Two firms are current-CEO interlocked if a current CEO from firm A sits on the board of firm B and a current CEO of firm B sits on the board of firm A. The other measures of interlock are also reciprocal arrangements but for different subsets of employees: 2. current-employee includes any current employees (including the CEOs), 3. retired-CEO only includes retired CEOs, 4. retired-employee includes any retired individuals including the CEOs, 5. any-CEO includes current or retired CEOs, and 6. any-employee is the most comprehensive measure and includes any current or retired employees including CEOs. The measures of compensation are (salary plus bonus), (salary plus bonus plus other compensation), and (total compensation). Other compensation includes such items as insurance policies, restricted shares that vested during the year, savings plan contributions, memberships in clubs etc. Total compensation is the sum of salary plus bonus plus other compensation plus exercised options. These compensation data are from Forbes magazine and are for 1992. This analysis is for the sample that includes complete data on board structure as well as complete data on compensation and other CEO and firm characteristics ($n = 602$). The interlocked fractions in the first column are basically the same if the entire board data are used. Asterisks represent statistically significant difference between mean compensation of interlocked and non-interlocked CEOs for given compensation and interlock measures at the 0.01(b), 0.05(c), and 0.10(d) levels.

banking, or other business relationships as not interlocked have an effect on the return to interlock' and also offers interesting and more plausible insight into the returns to the different measures of interlock. These columns present the results from three sets of linear regressions (for each of three independent variables), with the same independent variables as in columns 1, 3, and 5 except that firms are defined as not interlocked if they have documented customer/ supplier, banking, or other business relationships.

Redefining interlock in this way leaves only those firms with potentially the largest opportunity for agency problems. If the dual agency idea is correct, then this ought to yield higher returns to interlock. In all but one case, for the first two measures of compensation, the point estimate for the return to interlock is higher when firms with business relationships are considered to be not interlocked. It is also interesting to note that when interlocks are redefined

Table 8. Estimates of the return to interlock using several measures of interlock[a]

Interlock type	*ln(salary+bonus)*		*ln(salary+bonus+other)*		*ln(total compensation)*	
	Standard interlock definition (1)	*Business relationships considered not interlocked (2)*	*Standard interlock definition (3)*	*Business relationships considered not interlocked (4)*	*Standard interlock definition (5)*	*Business relationships considered not interlocked (6)*
1. Current-CEO	0.068 (0.793)	0.158 (1.528)	0.039 (0.413)	0.130 (1.134)	0.004 (0.032)	–0.028 (0.177)
2. Current-employee	0.096 (1.356)	0.159 (1.794)	0.119 (1.523)	0.174[c] (1.764)	0.014 (0.126)	–0.034 (0.247)
3. Retired-CEO	0.079 (0.812)	0.104 (1.026)	0.042 (0.392)	0.065 (0.574)	–0.047 (0.317)	–0.004 (0.026)
4. Retired-employee	0.078 (1.090)	0.076 (0.982)	0.109 (1.381)	0.111 (1.297)	0.085 (0.767)	0.070 (0.590)
5. Any-CEO	0.089 (1.282)	0.139[c] (1.823)	0.054 (0.700)	0.104 (1.235)	0.007 (0.065)	–0.010 (0.087)
6. Any-employee	0.092 (1.583)	0.116[c] (1.805)	0.142[b] (2.204)	0.166[b] (2.309)	0.060 (0.665)	0.045 (0.448)

[a]The dependent variables in each column are, respectively, ln(salary plus bonus), ln(salary plus bonus plus other compensation) and ln(total compensation). Other compensation includes such items as insurance policies, restricted shares that vested during the year, savings plan contributions, memberships in clubs, etc. Total compensation is the sum of salary plus bonus plus other compensation plus exercised options. These salary data are from Forbes magazine and are for 1992. All specifications also control for 20 industry indicator variables, age of the CEO and its square, seniority of the CEO in the firm and its square, seniority of the CEO as CEO and its square, ln(firm value), stock return in 1991, and the number of directors on the board. The first measure of interlock is 1. current-CEO interlock. Two firms are current-CEO interlocked if a current CEO from firm A sits on the board of firm B and the current CEO of firm B sits on the board of firm A. The other measures of interlock are also reciprocal arrangements but for different subsets of employees: 2. current-employee includes any current employees (including the CEOs), 3. retired-CEO only includes retired CEOs, 4. retired-employee includes any retired individuals including the CEOs, 5. any-CEO includes current or retired CEOs, and 6. any-employee is the most comprehensive measure and includes any current or retired employees including CEOs. This is the subset of data for which information is available on customer/supplier, banking, and other business relationships. b = significant at 0.05, c = significant at 0.10. There are 602 observations. (t-statistics are in parentheses).

in this way (for the first two dependent variables) the CEO interlock coefficients are higher relative to the employee interlock coefficients than before, and the current interlock coefficients are higher relative to the retired than before. This is consistent with the dual agency hypothesis.

Concluding comments

This chapter empirically studies corporate boards with reciprocal interlocking relationships and has several findings. First, it documents that there is a substantial amount of board interlocking. For example, roughly 20% of all boards are in situations where at least one current or retired employee of firm A is on the board of firm B and *vice versa*. The paper also shows that there is a significant amount of interlocking among current and even retired employees, although this is not as frequent as 20%.

The paper also shows that board interlocks may be due to agency problems in firms although the evidence certainly is not conclusive. The results of the simulations using the 1992 data suggest that interlock does not happen by chance. Directors interlock much more often than they would have had they been assigned randomly to board positions. This, however, is only a necessary condition for cronyism by directors and is not sufficient evidence to imply that directors are acting against the interests of shareholders. There seems to be other evidence that interlock may lead to agency conflicts. Although the difference is not significant, the fraction of interlocked firms to adopt poison pills and anti-takeover amendments is higher than the fraction of non-interlocked firms. It is also true that although several of the interlocks can be explained by business relationships, a substantial fraction remain unexplained. Also, interlock cannot be explained by management ownership. Other evidence in favor of the 'cronyism' hypothesis exists. Agrawal and Walkling (1994) suggest that takeover bids are more likely to occur in industries where CEOs have positive abnormal compensation, suggesting perhaps that new management can run the firm more efficiently. Also there is some evidence that the return to interlock is falling over time (Hallock (1997) shows that the return to interlock was significantly higher in 1976 than in 1992) which might suggest that recent attempts to open-up the process of executive salary determination are helping to curb cronyism.

Directors, on the other hand, may serve on each other's boards simply because they are known by one another to be of high quality. In fact, controlling for additional unobservables of CEOs that may be correlated with management ability suggests this may be true (see Hallock, 1997). In addition, if it were the case that interlock really did mean that CEOs, in collusion with directors, were extracting rents from the firm, then we might expect lower profits and returns from interlocked firms. This is not the case.

Finally, previous study of the compensation of Chief Executive Officers has excluded detailed analysis of the group which actually sets CEO pay, the board of directors. This work uses the sample of the composition of the boards of directors of America's largest firms as well as information on CEO compensation and firm characteristics for a number of years to test the hypothesis that CEOs who are reciprocally interlocked with other CEOs via their boards of directors can raise their wages above those of their counterparts who are not interlocked. It demonstrates that interlocked CEOs earn, on average, significantly higher wages than non-interlocked CEOs. After controlling for firm and CEO characteristics, this pay gap is reduced dramatically. However, when considering only those types of interlocks which are most likely to be symptomatic of agency problems, there does appear to be some evidence of a positive return to CEO pay for CEOs who interlock.

Acknowledgements

I am grateful to Sherrilyn Billger, John Core and Arthur Rosenbloom for comments.

References

Agrawal, A. and R. Walkling (1994). Executive careers and compensation surrounding takeover bids. *Journal of Finance*, **49**, 985–1014.

Arreglado, E.R. *Top Executive Compensation*: 1993 Edition. The Conference Board.

Baker, G., M. Gibbs and B. Holmstrom (1993). Hierarchies and compensation: a case study. *European Economic Review*, **37**, 366-378.

Baker, G., M.C. Jensen and K.J. Murphy (1988). Compensation and incentives: practice vs. theory. *Journal of Finance*, **18**, 593–616.

Bearden, J. and B. Mintz (1985). Regionality and integration in the American interlock network. In: F.N. Stockman, R. Ziegler and J. Scott (eds). *Networks of Corporate Power*. Polity Press, Cambridge, 234–249.

Belliveau, M.A., C.A. O'Reilly III and J.B. Wade (1996). Social capital at the top: the effects of social similarity and status on CEO compensation. *Academy Management Journal*, **39**, 1568–1593.

Bizjak, J.M., J.A. Brickley and J. Coles (1993). Stock-based incentive compensation and investment behavior. *Journal of Accounting and Economics*, **16**, 349–372.

Bowen, W.G. (1994). *Inside the Boardroom*. John Wiley & Sons, New York.

Bunting, D. and J. Barbour (1971). Interlocking directorates in large American corporations, 1896–1964. *Business History Review*, **45**, 317–35.

Ciscel, D.H. (1974). Determinants of executive compensation. *Southern Economic Journal*, **40**, 613–17.

Ciscel, D.H. and T.M. Carroll (1980). The determinants of executive salaries: an econometric survey. *Review of Economics and Statistics*, **62**, 7–13.

Coughlan, A.T. and R.M. Schmidt (1985). Executive compensation, management turnover, and firm performance: an empirical investigation. *Journal of Accounting and Economics*, **7**, 43–66.

DiNardo, J., K. Hallock and J.-S. Pischke (1997). *Unions and Managerial Pay*. NBER Working Paper 6318.

Directory of Corporate Affiliations (1992). National Register Publishing.

Dooley, P.C. (1969). The interlocking directorate. *American Economic Review*, **59**, 314–323.

Ehrenberg, R.G. and G.T. Milkovich (1987). Compensation and firm performance. In: M.M. Kleiner, R.N. Block, M. Roomkin and S.W. Salsburg (eds), *Human Resources and the Performance of the Firm*. Industrial Relations Research Association, 87–122.

Fama, E. (1980). Agency problems and the theory of the firm. *Journal of Political Economy*, **88**, 288–307.

Gibbons, R. and K.J. Murphy (1990). Relative performance evaluation of chief executive officers. *Industrial and Labor Relations Review*, **43**, 30s–51s.

Gibbons, R. and K.J. Murphy (1992). Optimal incentive contracts in the presence of career concerns: theory and evidence. *Journal of Political Economy*, **100**, 468–505.

Hall, B. and J. Liebman (1997). *Are CEOs really paid like bureaucrats?* NBER Working paper 6213.

Hallock, K. (1997). Reciprocally interlocking boards of directors and executive compensation. *Journal of Financial and Quantitative Analysis*, **32**, 331–344.

Hallock, K. (1998). Layoffs, top executive pay, and firm performance. *American Economic Review* **88**.

Hallock, K. and P. Oyer (1997). *What Have You Done For Me Lately? Executive Compensation and the Timing of Corporate Performance.* Working Paper, University of Illinois and Northwestern University.

Hermalin, B.E. and M.S. Weisbach (1988). The determinants of board composition. *Rand Journal of Economics*, **19**, 589–606.

Holmstrom, B. (1979). Moral hazard and observability. *Bell Journal of Economics*, **10**, 74–91.

Jensen, M.C. and W.H. Meckling (1976). Theory of the firm: managerial behavior, agency costs and ownership structure. *Journal of Financial Economics*, **3**, 305–360.

Jensen, M.C. and K.J. Murphy (1990). Performance pay and top management incentives. *Journal of Political Economy*, **98**, 225–264.

Kaplan, S.N. (1994). Top executives, turnover, and firm performance in Germany *Journal of Law, Economics, and Organization*, **10**, 142–159.

Kaplan, S.N. and B.A. Minton (1994). Appointments of outsiders to Japanese boards: determinants and implications for managers. *Journal of Financial Economics*, **36**, 225–258.

Lambert, R.A. and D.F. Larcker (1988). An analysis of the use of accounting and market measures of performance in executive compensation contracts. *Journal of Accounting Research*, **25** (supplement), 85–129.

Lazear, E.P. and S. Rosen (1981). Rank-order tournaments as optimum labor contracts. *Journal of Political Economy*, **89**, 841–864.

Leonard, J.S. (1990). Executive pay and firm performance. *Industrial and Labor Relations Review*, **43**, 13s–29s.

Lewellen, W. and B. Huntsman (1970). Managerial pay and corporate performance. *American Economic Review*, **60**, 710–720.

Main, B.G.M., C.A. O'Reilly III and J. Wade (1995). The CEO, the board of directors and executive compensation: economic and psychological perspectives. *Industrial and Corporate Change*, **4**, 293–332.

Masson, R.T. (1971). Executive motivations, earnings, and consequent equity performance. *Journal of Political Economy*, **79**, 1278–1292.

Mayers, D. and C.W. Smith Jr. (1992). Executive compensation in the life insurance industry. *The Journal of Business*, **65**, 51–71.

Million Dollar Directory (1992). Dunns Marketing Services.

Mintz, B. and M. Schwartz (1981). Interlocking directorates and interest group formation. *American Sociological Review*, **46**, 851–869.

Mizruchi, M.S. (1982). *The American Corporate Network, 1904–1974*, Sage Publications.

Mizruchi, M.S. and L.B. Stearns (1988). A longitudinal study of the formation of interlocking directorates. *Administrative Science Quarterly*, **33**, 194–210.

Murphy, K.J. (1985). Corporate performance and managerial remuneration: an empirical analysis. *Journal of Accounting and Economics*, **7**, 11–42.

Murphy, K.J. (1986). Incentives, learning, and compensation: a theoretical and empirical investigation of managerial labor contracts. *Rand Journal of Economics*, **17**, 59–76.

Newman, H.A. and D.W. Wright (1995). *Compensation Committee Composition and its Influence on CEO Compensation Practices.* Working Paper, University of Michigan.

O'Reilly, C.A. III, B.G. Main and G.S. Crystal (1988). CEO compensation as tournament and social comparison: a tale of two theories. *Administrative Science Quarterly*, **33**, 257–274.
Pennings, J.M. (1980). *Interlocking Directorates.* Jossey-Bass Publishers.
Rediker, K.J. and A. Seth (1995). Boards of directors and substitution effects of alternative governance mechanisms. *Strategic Management Journal*, **16**, 85–99.
Rees, A. (1992). The tournament as a model for executive compensation. *Journal of Post Keynesian Economics*, **14**, 567–571.
Roberts, D. (1956). A general theory of executive compensation based on statistically tested propositions. *Quarterly Journal of Economics*, **70**, 270–294.
Sloan, R. (1993). Accounting earnings and top executive compensation. *Journal of Accounting and Economics*, **16**, 349–372.
Standard and Poor's Register of Corporations, Directors, and Executives (1992). McGraw Hill.
Weisbach, M.S. (1988). Outside directors and CEO turnover. *Journal of Financial Economics*, **20**, 431–460.
Who's Who in Finance and Industry, 27th edn (1992). Marquis.
Williamson, O.E. (1963). Managerial discretion and business behavior. *American Economic Review*, **53**, 1032–1057.
Yermack, D. (1996). Higher market valuation of companies with a small board of directors. *Journal of Financial Economics*, **40**, 185–211.

ARTHUR H. ROSENBLOOM
Leonard N. Stern School of Business

6. Discussion of Hallock paper on reciprocal interlocks

My approach to papers on matters such as board of directors interlocks proceeds partially from my position as an adjunct professor but mostly from the vantage point of a full time practitioner who, among other things, advises boards on the reasonableness of executive pay. I view such scholarship from three perspectives. First, in the search for the truth that is the subject of the paper, I apply the classical scholarly model; do the approaches taken have the requisite intellectual rigour, was the sample well chosen, is the statistical analysis persuasive, etc. In this respect, apart from some methodological issues developed below, I believe Professor Hallock's analysis is generally persuasive. My second perspective is a policy one. Since we deal here with a real world phenomenon, does the paper develop insights that might be useful at a policy level? Do its findings argue for a need for legislative, administrative or judicial reform? In my view, Professor Hallock's conclusions suggest no need for such reform. Finally, as a practitioner, might the paper's findings allow me to bring new insights to my clients or cause me to modify the kind of advice I give them on the matters that are the subject of the paper? In this instance too, I believe the answer is no.

Recognizing that the choice tends to stack the desk against the findings, is it reasonable to assume that the directors in the sample are the entire universe of directors? While one understands the need for simplifying assumptions, does this one conform sufficiently closely to reality to make it a useful one? In my view, it does not.

An underlying assumption is that interlocks are likely to occur with equal frequency within an industry as not. However, is it likely to be the case as Professor Hallock hypothesizes, that interlocks within an industry will occur with the same frequency as interlocks involving directors from different industries? It would appear that fear of advertent or inadvertent misappropriation of information learned by a board member of a company who is an officer/director of a company in the same industry would make such interlocks the exception and not the rule. As a policy question, it might be interesting to inquire why the Clayton Act which Professor Hallock describes as precluding intra-industry board interlocks is, by his account, so little brought to bear to

J. Carpenter and D. Yermack (eds.), Executive Compensation and Shareholder Value, 77–79.

bar such interlocks. Might it be the fact that there is no demonstrable evidence suggesting that intraindustry interlocks restrain trade?

As to customer/supplier/banking and other business relationships, if the data is available, should the methodology not attempt to distinguish between material and non-material relationships say as a percentage of annual revenues? I would clearly be more concerned about material business relationships and less so about less material ones.

With respect to performance, Professor Hallock hypothesizes that interlocks could be the result of agency problems and suggests at least the possibility of crony laden boards rubber stamping management's decisions to the shareholder's detriment. However, the data adduced in the paper is as follows. First, investor returns are immaterially different in interlocked vs non-interlocked forms. As a practitioner I ask if shareholder wealth creation is not adversely affected, where's the beef? Second, since there is a statistically insignificant relationship between firms with lower returns and poison pills, anti-takeover amendments or golden parachutes, Now for a closer look at Professor Hallock's paper: it appears difficult to sustain the assertion of an agency problem

The data, I believe, oversimplify pay for performance analysis. It is not just the stock market return of the firm developed by Professor Hallock that counts, but how well the firm has compared to its peer firms in growth (revenues and earnings) investment returns (ROA/ROE), liquidity, leverage and in non-financial terms (e.g., developing successor management). Our work in executive compensation litigation (either in an IRS reasonable compensation or a shareholder derivative lawsuit context) suggests (as does the case law) that reasonableness of executive compensation is precisely about what the executive is worth to the company and its shareholders.

As to whether reciprocal interlocks involving CEOs or non-CEOs of companies "give rise to unusual opportunities to increase each other's compensation", I suggest that research should expand on previous work and be directed to whether such persons sit on the compensation committees of such boards, for that is where the serious work on compensation is usually undertaken. Further assuming a predisposition to mutually back scratch in compensation, such collusion is subject to the override by the majority of the board who have no such interlocks. In that connection, Professor Hallock's one board member model has no real world counterpart. In the final analysis the data offer no evidence that the interlocking directors so collude. To do so, one needs to establish the same quantum of proof as that required to prove adultery – inclination plus opportunity.

Professor Hallock's data in Table 7, suggesting that current CEO interlocked firms pay their CEO's an average of 32.63% more than non-current CEO interlocked firms, is quite interesting and bears further study. It would, I believe, benefit from a pay for performance analysis to determine the reason for this phenomenon. To do so, in my view requires a deeper analysis of total compensation to include the value of equity incentives, vested or not, this producing a total compensation figure which recognizes the material impact of the equity incentives which today constitute such a large part of total executive compensation. The analysis involves, through Black Scholes, or other models such as the Shelton formula, measuring the fair market value of the equity incentives.

PART THREE

BRIAN G.M. MAIN
University of Edinburgh
The David Hume Institute

7. The rise and fall of executive share options in Britain

INTRODUCTION

A useful way in which to examine the British approach to top executive pay is through the use made of executive share options as a component of the pay package. In marked contrast with developments in the USA, institutional investors have taken a leading role in conditioning the type of pay package that is possible for Britain's top executives. This intervention can be seen as leading initially to an expansion in the use of executive share options but more recently to a marked decline in their use. In general, it is far from clear that such intervention has been particularly productive. This paper attempts to trace these developments and, using the actual histories of 62 FTSE-100 companies, offers an empirical evaluation of the effectiveness of option-based incentive pay packages vs. the more recently favored share-based packages.

In discussing the rise and fall in popularity of executive share options in Britain, we first trace the post-1984 rise in popularity. There then follows an account of how the Cadbury Committee and, in particular, the Greenbury Committee set in train forces that have brought about a marked reversal in this trend. The Preliminary Report of the Hampel Committee is also discussed at this stage. Consideration is then given to the practice of other European countries in utilizing executive share options, before offering some rudimentary empirical evidence concerning the relative efficacy of executive share options as compared to their proposed replacement, the Long-Term Incentive Plan, or 'Ltip'. We conclude with a brief summary and some ideas for future policy.

I am grateful to Trevor Buck and Alistair Bruce for useful discussion and comments during the preparation of this paper, and to John Carney of Towers-Perrin for providing invaluable information and insights. The paper also benefited from comments received at the *Conference on Executive Compensation*, New York University Salomon Center. Remaining errors are my own.

J. Carpenter and D. Yermack (eds.), Executive Compensation and Shareholder Value, 83–113.

THE FOUR TIMES EMOLUMENTS RULE AND OTHER CONSTRAINTS

Until 1984, the use of executive share options among British companies was far from common. Unrestricted (company wide) save as you earn share option schemes did exist but were of modest maximum value (£50 per month maximum under the 1980 Finance Act). Some grants of options were made to executives through restricted schemes and these had been encouraged by the incoming conservative government of 1979, but they were not particularly popular. They held no tax advantage, as any resulting capital gains were taxed as income tax (the top marginal rate of income tax was 83% until 1979, when it was reduced to 60%).

In an attempt to further encourage pay for performance among senior managers, the Finance Act 1984 introduced the notion of 'approved share option schemes'. As will be seen below, the label approved carried normative overtones that have had far reaching consequences which might have been avoided had a more neutral term such as eligible or qualified been used. Approved schemes were discretionary in the sense that a company could include only those employees that it wished. Such schemes also offered a substantial tax advantage, with any subsequent capital gains on exercise being taxed at the capital gains rate of tax (then 30%) as opposed to being taxed as income (where the top marginal rate, although reduced, was still 60%). In addition, under approved schemes any tax liability arose only on the final disposition of the shares rather than at the time of option exercise. In order to limit the tax expenditure consequences of allowing income to be taxed at the capital gains rate (30%) as opposed to the income tax rate (60% for most of the executives involved), a limit of four times emoluments was set on the face value of shares that could be held under option at any one time, emoluments being defined here to include base and bonus pay but excluding the cash equivalent of any payments in kind. The conditions of a minimum vesting period of 3 years and a maximum option life of 10 years were also imposed. Satisfaction of these and various other conditions brought approved status and favorable tax treatment. The value of executive share options granted to executives is not liable to employers' national insurance contributions (a 10.4% payroll tax). In contrast to the USA, however, gains realized by executives on exercise of their options are not tax deductible by the company.

The overwhelming majority of executive share option schemes proposed for the approval of shareholders and the Inland Revenue involved honouring the options when exercised by the issue of new shares, rather than by acquiring the necessary shares through purchase in the open market (by subscription rather than by acquisition). Accounting standards did not (and do not) require recognition of such an issue of new shares as an expenditure, thereby protecting stated earnings. This course of action sacrifices a tax deduction, but the prime concern that these schemes induced among the institutions (who hold the overwhelming majority of shares) was not with regard to this missed opportunity but focused on the consequent equity dilution that occurs through the issue of new shares at below market price.

The Institutional Shareholders Committee (ISC), the National Association of Pension Funds (NAPF) and the Association of British Insurers (ABI) were all involved in codifying governance behavior during the 1980s, but it was undoubtedly the ABI which took the lead in terms of executive share options. The ABI essentially used the 1984 Inland Revenue rules for approved share option schemes and incorporated most of their features into what became the ABI guidelines for both approved and non-approved schemes. The ABI code did introduce the notion of 'super options' in the form of a second simultaneously held tranche of options worth a further four times emoluments. This second tranche was, however, required to have a minimum vesting period of 5 years and a performance hurdle that demanded earnings per share (EPS) growth over a 5 year period that was at least as good as upper quartile FTSE-100 out turns over the comparable period. Few companies utilized this second form of share option.

Not only were approved executive share option schemes widely and enthusiastically adopted in Britain's board rooms (Figure 1), but when executives subsequently chose to exercise their options (usually within a year or so of the 3-year vesting period having passed) pressure arose for further tranches of options to be issued. In May 1988 the ABI duly conceded by relaxing conditions so that options could be reissued to an executive once the original tranche was exercised. A modest performance hurdle was imposed here – of having attained "a significant improvement in the performance of the company over the 2–3 years preceding the regrant". It was also required that

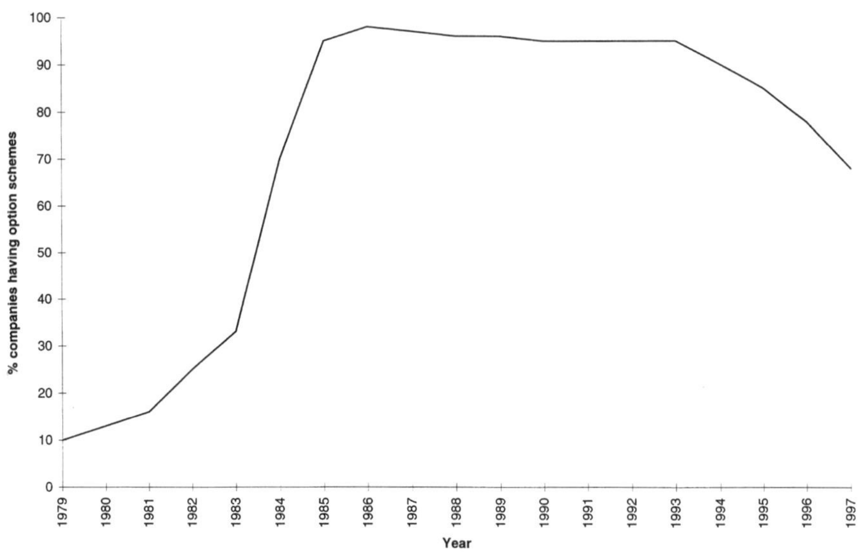

Figure 1. Executive share options: UK 1979–1997

the scheme be administered and supervised by a remuneration committee consisting wholly or mainly of non-executive directors.

In the 1988 Finance Act the government reduced the top rate of income tax to 40% and harmonized capital gains tax with an individual's marginal rate of income tax. This removed almost all of the tax advantage to operating an approved share option scheme. The benefits remaining included the possibility of delaying any tax due until the underlying shares were actually sold (rather than at time of option exercise) and the use of the annual capital gains allowance. In reality, almost all executives exercised and sold at the same time, and the tax shield of the annual capital gains allowance, even if not used towards other personal investments, amounted to a modest £6000 or thereabouts. The advantage of continuing approved tax status for an options scheme was, therefore, trivial. But by this time the ABI guidelines had assumed a statute like status and the four times emoluments rule continued to be implemented.

In 1991 (with effect from January 1992) the government attempted to encourage companies to offer company-wide, non-discretionary share option schemes by making their existence a condition of a new privilege to be extended to approved executive share option schemes. This new and advantageous condition permitted the issue of options with a strike price at a discount of as much as 15% on the prevailing market price. The ABI reacted quickly, making it a condition that options issued at such a discount should be subject to a 5-year vesting period and a performance hurdle of growth in EPS of "at least equal to the retail price index plus 2%". In fact such discounts were rarely used.

By this stage, however, very few companies deviated from the strict interpretation of the ABI guidelines. The guidelines themselves retained their basic outline, although with mounting public criticism of top executive pay there was a tightening of conditions introduced in revised versions. For example, whereas while before replacement options can be issued the condition is still demanded of "a sustained improvement in the performance of the company over the 2–3 years preceding the further grant", now a further condition on exercise of definitive performance criteria is required. Specific examples of evidence of the sustained improvement in the underlying performance of the group are given by the ABI. These include "earnings per share with a 2% per annum growth in excess of inflation over a 3 year period". Reference is also made to comparative measures such as EPS, net asset value per share, total shareholder return, or share price – all relative to an appropriate comparator group of companies. The ABI guidelines currently in force (issued February 1995) still, however, retain the imprint of the 1984 Inland Revenue regulations for approved share option schemes.

During the 1990s there has been mounting public concern and outcry regarding the apparent unending rise of top executive pay (particularly among recently privatized utilities). This trend can be seen in Figure 2 which maps base plus bonus pay for the highest paid director in a sample of traded UK companies over the period 1969 to 1995. Although this shows that pay can fall

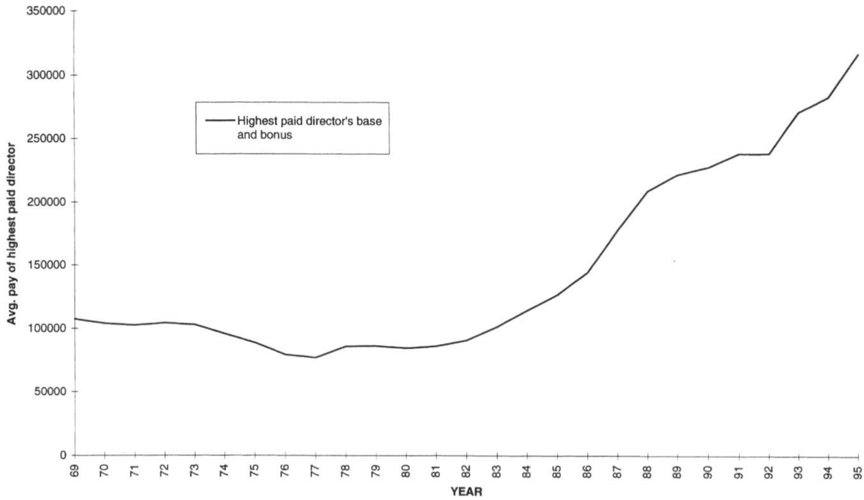

Figure 2. Average pay of highest paid director – UK 1969–1995 (in £1989)

as well as rise, the recent trend has been markedly upwards. While no political party has suggested direct intervention in the matter of determining top executive pay, the Labour Party (1994) did campaign for the abolition of tax privileges on executive share options. Consequent on the report of the Greenbury Committee in 1995 (of which more below), the Chancellor of the Exchequer essentially conceded the point by abolishing all remaining tax privileges with effect from July 1995 (reintroducing a similar scheme in the subsequent November's Budget, but with an allowed maximum of £30,000 worth of shares under option, this being of such modest proportions as to be of little or no interest to senior executives). In a recent paper, Conyon *et al.* (1995, p.714) suggest that under certain circumstances "one needs genuinely to discuss the case for legally binding regulation of methods of setting executive compensation packages". While this argument has found little support, it is argued below that the existing codes of practice following from the ABI, the Cadbury Committee, the Greenbury Committee and the Hampel Committee already place the operation of top executive pay in a regulatory strait jacket.

The contrast with the USA is quite marked. There the regulatory authorities, as opposed to the institutional investors and other ad hoc bodies, have sought greater transparency in reporting while leaving boards and their compensation committees to decide the detail of executive pay structure. The regulatory authorities in the form of the Securities and Exchange Commission (SEC) and the Financial and Accounting Standards Board (FASB) have taken the lead in these matters. The SEC (1993) enjoyed considerable success in extending and deepening the reporting detail concerning executive remuneration awards made to the top five officers of a corporation, with the requirement that this reporting be set in the context of recent company performance. In the case of FASB (1993), however, there was a considerable backlash to its proposals to extend the reporting and recognition of the executive share option component of executive pay. In the face of implacable opposition from the corporations themselves, the FASB proposals were to all intents and purposes defeated (FASB, 1994). Institutional investors in the form of Calpers and other organizations have taken an acute interest in the implementation of company executive pay policy but without attempting to impose any general rules or guidelines.

In the UK, the running has been made by non-statutory bodies such as the ABI or, as we shall see below, in private sector initiatives through well-intentioned committees of business people, albeit backed by the power of the listings regulations of the London Stock Exchange (the 'Yellow Book'). The prime example is the Cadbury Committee (1992) which was set up by the Financial Reporting Council and the accounting profession to look at corporate governance after some spectacular and unexpected company failures (e.g. Coloroll and Polly Peck). Initially it had no specific brief to examine top executive pay, but very ably extended its considerations to embrace this topic in response to increasingly critical press coverage of top pay awards. As we shall see below, there was a generally positive reception to the Cadbury Code, but it was the Greenbury Committee (1995), set up by the Confederation of British Industry (CBI) at the behest of the Cabinet Office, that most dramatically extended the regulatory environment in terms of procedures, reporting, and pay design. Most recently the Hampel Committee (1997) has issued a preliminary report that evaluates the impact of both Cadbury and Greenbury and attempts to provide some consolidation. We shall now turn to examine the codes issued by these committees as they impact upon the determination and reporting of top executive pay.

The committees' progress

Although not specifically set up to examine top pay, the Cadbury Committee Report (1992) contains the following pertinent recommendations:

- boards should include at least three non-executive directors of whom at least two should be judged independent;
- non-executives should be able to take expert advice at the company's expense;
- non-executives should be selected through a formal process involving the whole board, and good practice suggests the use of a nominations committee with a majority of non-executives;
- full and clear disclosure of emoluments (including pension and share options) of the chairman and the highest paid UK director, with any

performance element of salary reported separately and the basis on which performance is measured explained;

- executive directors' contracts should not exceed three years without shareholders' approval;
- executive directors' pay should be determined by a remuneration committee made up wholly or mainly of non-executive directors.

Enforcement of these conditions is by means of an audited statement in the annual report which either claims compliance or gives reasons for non-compliance. Listing on the London Stock Exchange is conditional upon the appearance of such an audited statement.

The Greenbury Committee Report (1995) took matters further by recommending that:

- remuneration committees should decide executive pay, should comprise entirely of non-executive (independent) directors, and have access to professional advisers;
- the remuneration committee chairman to account directly to shareholders through a detailed report on remuneration policy in the annual report and accounts, and to be available at the AGM to answer questions;
- full details of all elements of remuneration for each individual director to be reported, and to include detail on share options (in conformance with the Accounting Standards Board's recommendations) and pension entitlements. Pensions to be calculated on base pay only and not on bonuses or long-term incentive schemes;
- service contracts in excess of one year to be disclosed and justified;
- remuneration packages to be designed to attract, retain and motivate directors but to avoid paying excessively (upper limits on bonuses and part payment in the form of shares encouraged);
- traditional share option schemes to be weighed against other kinds of long-term incentive scheme, and payouts under all long-term incentive schemes to be subject to challenging performance criteria;
- options not to be issued at a discount and gains from option schemes to be taxed as income at exercise rather than as capital gains at disposal;
- grants of options should normally be phased over time rather than made in one large block;
- privatized utilities to review comprehensively their existing remuneration packages;
- the London Stock Exchange to enforce compliance with the Code through its listing requirements.

The report explicitly recognizes that, while there is a market for executive talent, this market is imperfect and remuneration committees have "a wide range of discretion in setting levels and forms of remuneration" (section 6.4). While highlighting the behavior of recently privatized utilities, the report makes the general observation on recent developments in directors' remuneration that "companies mostly deal with Directors' remuneration in a sensible and responsible manner" (section 1.9) while going on to add that "there have been, in our view, mistakes and misjudgments" (section 1.11).

The Accounting Standards Board (ASB) recommendations on the reporting of executive share options alluded to in the Greenbury Code were delivered in the form of an Urgent Issues Task Force Information Sheet No. 11 (1994). This stopped considerably short of the FASB recommendation for the USA, which had called for explicit evaluation and recognition of the expense of share options. The ASB effectively recommended only that certain raw data be provided on the tranches of share options held by individual directors. The nature of the data to be disclosed is such that interested parties can, with the addition of some recent measures of company share performance, compute their own approximate valuations of option holdings by executives. Thus details such as the number of options issued, strike price, date of issue and expiry date are to be provided.

The London Stock Exchange responded to the Greenbury Committee by first circulating a consultative document in July 1995 and then in October amending its listing rules (in Amendment 6: section 12.43) with effect from 31 December 1995. These new listing rules of the London Stock Exchange (the Yellow Book) add regulatory enforcement[1] to the Cadbury and Greenbury Codes. By and large the detail of the Cadbury and Greenbury Codes survives.

In addition to recommending performance hurdles for the exercise of executive share options, Greenbury gives a clear steer away from option schemes: "these schemes, at least in their traditional form, also have draw backs" (Greenbury, 1995, 6.28). The report goes on to state that "the other forms of incentive scheme which should be weighed against share options typically reward Directors with a predetermined number of shares or cash amounts, rather than share options" (6.31), and adds that "schemes along these lines may be as effective, or more so, than improved share options schemes in linking rewards to performance" (6.32). This message seems to have found its mark.

A recent report by New Bridge Street Consultants (1996, p4) indicates that "even before Greenbury expressed a guarded preference for alternative plans over the traditional executive share option scheme" companies were switching out of option schemes and into Ltips. A substantial number of the FTSE-100 companies (e.g. British Gas, BT, Courtalds, Prudential, and Reuters) have given up their executive share option schemes altogether and as many as 58 of

[1] Some commentators (e.g. Robertson, 1995) have complained that this extra regulatory burden has imposed significant compliance costs, particularly upon smaller companies.

these same FTSE-100 companies had adopted alternative long-term incentive plans, although sometimes alongside existing option schemes. The majority of these newly introduced Ltips are share based (analogous in some ways to restricted stock schemes as operated in the USA). The trend to replacing share option schemes is expected to continue. We shall examine the findings of the New Bridge Street Consultants report in more detail later.

In yet another private enterprise initiative, the Hampel Committee, charged with reviewing the implementation of the Cadbury and the Greenbury Committees' recommendations, issued a preliminary report in August 1997. This introduced few changes, seeking, in the main, to clarify and simplify. In the area of executive pay the following recommendations of the report are relevant here:

- Remuneration committees should merely recommend pay awards to the board which should then approve or disapprove them.
- Remuneration committees are to use their judgment in devising incentive pay schemes appropriate to the individual circumstances of the company, while attempting to make the statement on remuneration policy that appears in the annual report more informative rather than obfuscating it with detail.
- The remuneration needed to attract and retain executive directors of the required calibre will be largely determined by the market.
- Intercompany comparisons and remuneration surveys should be used with caution.
- Terms and conditions for early departure of executives (excluding misconduct) to be agreed in advance and to avoid any duty to mitigate loss being imposed on the executive.
- Two year service contracts while not general should be acceptable in certain circumstances.
- Shareholders should expect to approve incentive schemes extending over more than one year or leading to equity dilution, but there should be no shareholder approval of individual pay packages.
- The separation of chairman and chief executive should not be a firm rule, but departures should be justified. In all cases a lead non-executive should be identified.
- Non-executives should continue to be barred from participation in share option schemes but payment in the form of company shares should now be permitted.
- Nomination committees should be required, not just recommended.

Hampel, therefore, accepts the main conclusions of Cadbury and Greenbury while slightly redefining the role of the remuneration committee by restoring overarching responsibility on executive pay determination to the board itself, and allowing the Chairman to decide who speaks to what question at the AGM. Although it stresses the important role of non-executive directors (and independent non-executives), and indeed goes as far as recommending that a lead non-executive be identified, the report is an endorsement of the unitary board structure – a unitary board acting in a collective and collegial manner.

The dual board structure prevalent in other European countries is, therefore, rejected, but it is not only in board structure that other countries in Europe differ from Britain. The approach to incentive structure of top executive pay seems to be somewhat less developed elsewhere in Europe than in Britain. The following section attempts to provide an overview of share option use in Europe.

The wider European view

Information on the use of executive share options across Europe is available in a recent survey by Monks Partnership (1996) and summarized in Table 1. Unfortunately, because of the nature of the survey, this information tends to reflect the practice of regional headquarters of US and UK owned multinationals in those European countries rather than provide a comprehensive overview of the practices of all companies in those countries. But given that practice in affiliates is influenced not only by policy at headquarters but also by local practice, the information, which is summarized in Table 1, may be of some interest, although the important caveat on coverage must be borne in mind.

The general picture that emerges is one of fairly universal use of annual bonus schemes at both the managing director (CEO) level and the executive director level. In terms of longer term incentives, however, there seems to be a marked variation in practice. UK practice, as discussed above, is to grant executives options over a value of shares defined in terms of multiples of base and bonus pay (for senior executives usually four-times). In Dutch, French and German parent companies, while the grant of options is reasonably widespread, they are not accepted as a major component of pay. In the case of Germany it is well known that domestic companies have not utilized executive share options until recently. The opposition in the supervisory board (and widespread press discussion) when Deutsche Bank moved to introduce even a modest share option type scheme for its senior management makes this clear. Other German companies such as BHF-Bank, Continental, Daimler-Benz, Deutsche Telekom and Siemens are also prepared to move in this direction. The German Stock Law is currently being changed in ways that will facilitate the use of executive share options, obviating the need to rely on a somewhat convoluted use of bond warrants. Until recently such innovations were widely regarded as unthinkable.

Table 1. Characteristics of long-term incentives across Europe (Caveat: Reflects behaviour of UK and US affiliates)

	% of Managing directors with:				*% of Directors with:*			
Country (No. of companies)	*Annual bonus*	*Share options*	*Ltips*	*(No. of positions)*	*Annual bonus*	*Share options*	*Ltips*	*(No. of positions)*
Austria (20)	100	79	7	(14)	86	50	2	(42)
Belgium (43)	96	75	4	(19)	90	53	2	(49)
Denmark (17)	85	46	7	(13)	90	44	0	(39)
Finland (10)	83	33	0	(6)	100	13	0	(23)
France (108)	90	58	13	(72)	84	41	7	(233)
Germany (72)	92	55	12	(49)	90	39	7	(111)
Greece (14)	82	55	9	(11)	78	39	11	(18)
Ireland (14)	100	71	0	(7)	100	59	0	(27)
Italy (47)	84	47	11	(31)	87	37	0	(128)
Netherlands (51)	97	59	15	(39)	96	30	9	(113)
Norway (14)	71	57	14	(7)	81	12	0	(26)
Portugal (19)	91	46	18	(11)	85	23	6	(48)
Spain (61)	95	48	12	(42)	93	29	7	(135)
Sweden (27)	90	55	0	(20)	80	33	0	(55)
Switzerland (21)	95	74	11	(19)	89	69	2	(45)
UK (557)	85	86	29	(508)	89	86	32	(1477)

Source: Abstracted from *Remuneration of Directors and Managers – Europe*, Monks Partnership Ltd. (1996). Data as of July1, 1996.

Among managing directors in the Monks' survey (reflecting affiliate practice), the median country has option usage of 59%. The range is from a low of 33% in Finland to a high of 86% in the UK. Among directors in general, the figures reveal a median option usage of 39%. Again the variation is wide, running from a low of 12% in Norway to a high of 86% in the UK. The UK figures would have been even higher were it not for the recent move away from options and towards Ltips.

A similarly wide variation is found for the utilization of Ltips, but with a generally lower level of usage overall. For managing directors there is a median figure of 11%. The range is from zero (for three countries) to a high of 29% (the UK). For directors in general the median is a modest two% usage. Only in the UK (32% usage) can Ltips be said to be anything but rare among directors. In six countries, they are not found at all in the companies surveyed.

Some of this variation in share option usage may reflect different tax treatment in the various regimes. But there is little marked hostility evident in the various tax codes. A more detailed discussion is available in Monks (1996) and for US schemes operating in Europe in Vesley and Shannon (1994). But some highlights are:

- In Austria share option gains are treated as income, although tax exemption can be claimed on up to $1,000 or so gains per year subject to a 5 year retention of the underlying shares. Gains on the stock itself are waived after a 12 month holding period.
- In Belgium $15,000 or so of option gains per year are tax exempt, subject to various conditions, including the retention of the share after option exercise for a further 2 years. Otherwise option gains are treated as income.
- In France up to $20,000 per year in option gains are tax free if the options are held for 5 years. Otherwise option gains are again treated as income and taxed at marginal rates of up to 54%, although exempt from social security tax which would bring the rate up to 66%. If held for 5 years or more then option gains in excess of $20,000 are subject to capital gains tax at 34.9%, thus making executive share options attractive to employees. In addition disclosure requirements and restrictions on personal holdings appear to be extremely lax.
- In Germany, with the exception of a modest tax exemption of $200 per year, option gains are treated as income, and taxed accordingly.
- In Holland there is an interesting departure from the normal convention of taxing share option gains on exercise. There the value of a share option grant is defined as 7.5% of the market value of the underlying shares, with the restriction that the strike price must be the market price at the time of grant. The options are subject to tax on the day they are granted and limited to a 5 year life. For company-wide qualifying share option schemes, there is a £750 per year disregard of this tax.
- In Ireland income tax relief on approved share option schemes was repealed in 1992. This left only the more modest if more general approved profit sharing schemes attracting tax privileges.
- In Spain option gains are taxed at income at the time when the option is exercised.
- In the UK, as explained above, executive share options are now essentially taxed as income at the time when the option is exercised. The £30,000 qualifying ceiling on shares under option that applies in the resurrected Inland Revenue approved share option scheme is of such modest proportions as to render it irrelevant to most senior executives. As shall be explained below, there has now been a significant and growing move away from executive share options into Ltips.

In summary, for most European countries considered here there are now only modest tax advantages to remunerating executives in the form of share options. Their attraction, therefore, rests in the incentive effects and their efficiency in this dimension as compared with alternative incentive schemes.

The European Union (1992) itself has attempted to encourage employee share participation through the issue of a relatively weak recommendation, but this was targeted at the general employee population rather than senior executives.

Share options versus Ltips

Options

It is our argument that the main problem with executive share options pre-Greenbury was that, owing to the way in which the ABI code of practice was put into effect, companies treated options as an automatic add-on to the remuneration package – an entitlement. In the overwhelming majority of cases, this tendency was reinforced by the failure to report or recognize the expense of executive share options in company accounts.

For most of the last decade, the award of options to executives was almost a matter of routine in many companies, with the meetings of the remuneration committee scheduled in such a way that one meeting would determine the bonus and hence total emoluments for the period just closed, and a following meeting would then compute the appropriate award of options that could be made in the light of this outturn (using the four times rule in an almost mechanistic way). It would appear that at no stage were executive share options considered as an integral part of the remuneration package whereby this long-term, quintessential performance-related component is traded off against a lower award of more immediate cash based pay. With such a recognition, then, in some companies and in some circumstances one would expect to see options as a major component of the remuneration package, thereby effecting a vigorous connection between pay and performance. Equally, in other circumstances one might expect options to play a more modest role. The post-1984 reality was that options assumed an almost constant proportion of cash based pay with little attention apparently given to the appropriate pay–performance leverage or the trade-off between one source of remuneration and the other. Using US data, Yermack (1995) presented empirical evidence that cast doubt on whether US companies were utilizing share options in ways that were at all consistent with what agency theory would predict.

Were a proactive approach to be adopted, a remuneration committee would need to have a feel for the value of the package of financial assets that they were awarding to the executive. The concept of valuing executive share options is, of course, not trivial. Conventional American and European options can be evaluated using variants of the Black-Scholes (1973) and Merton (1973) approach. Cox *et al.* (1979) offer an alternative and more flexible approach that has been widely developed among financial analysts. As Smith and Zimmerman (1976) point out, however, executive share options are not observed being traded in the market place. They also possess features that make them different from more conventional options: they have a much longer life (from 3 to 10 years as opposed to 9 months or so); they must be exercised or allowed to lapse as they cannot be traded to a third party; vesting of the ownership right to the option is uncertain for at least the first 3 years; and a corporate takeover can force early exercise. Yet another consideration is that there is a correlation between the probability of the executive remaining with the company through the vesting period and the probability of the option being worth exercising.

Noreen and Wolfson (1981) and Foster *et al.* (1991) argue that as a first approximation conventional valuation approaches such as Black-Scholes are adequate. Following the publication of the FASB draft exposure document, this question received a great deal of attention. A stream of high quality work, including Bey and Johnson (1994), Cuny and Jorion (1995), Hemmer *et al.* (1994, 1996), Jennergren and Naslund (1993), Huddart (1996), Huddart and Lang (1996), Mozes (1994), and Yermack (1995) among others, demonstrates the extent to which the special features of executive share options can be recognized. For example, Bey and Johnson (1994) computed that the impact of the non-transferability of executive share options is a significant one. Hemmer *et al.* (1996) and Huddart (1994) explored further the non-transferability aspect arguing that this, coupled with an inability to diversify the risk in any other way, leads executives to early exercise of their executive share options. Such a reaction should therefore be incorporated into any pricing formula, as it reduces the expense to the company of granting executive share options.

Huddart and Lang (1996) presented data drawn from the experience of over 50,000 employees and documented the importance of this early-exercise phenomenon. An argument was also put forward by Hemmer *et al.* (1996) that empirically firms tend to vary other components of executive pay to compensate for option risk. Jennergen and Naslund (1993) recommended the recognition of the exit of employees from the company before options have vested by multiplying the Black-Scholes option valuation by the probability of departure within the vesting period. Cuny and Jorion (1995) demonstrated that this practice leads to a downward bias in the valuation process owing to the inverse correlation of departure events and stock price movements. The bias is even greater when the stock option plan is designed with performance related vesting restrictions (a high performance leading more options to vest in the executive's favor). The two themes of early exercise and executive departure were brought together by Mozes (1994).

Somewhat ironically the general disquiet with executive share options that is evident in the Greenbury Report and in countless newspaper articles has little to do with these difficult concepts, but relates to a widespread feeling that executive share options represent 'something for nothing' and 'a one-way bet'. The feeling that they are neither earned nor sufficiently taxing of executive effort can be seen in the move by the ABI (and enforced by Greenbury) to place ever more severe performance hurdles both in terms of the issue of options and on the exercise of options. The view that options represent a one-way bet is manifested by arguments in favor of the imposition of stringent performance hurdles on the exercise of executive share options and, in a stronger version of the argument, for their replacement with more 'share-based' incentive schemes that are seen to have the ability to both decrease and increase in value.

Examples of several of these concerns can be found in the recent review by Conyon et al. (1995, pp. 706–7, p.712): " .. the granting of options confers substantial increases in wealth on executives and, probably more importantly, this part will only act as an incentive if the granting of options is linked to performance". "It is also true that, due to the volatility of share prices and the ability of the shareholder to pick the moment to sell, their initial value can be very large." "..potential gain is greater the more volatile the stock held and may well be unrelated to company performance." ".. the share price appreciation of the stock option will on average reflect the general appreciation of all stocks and so a certain part will offer a gain to the holder of the option which is not specific to the performance of the firm."

Similarly, in the press *The Economist* (August 16, 1997, p59) reported: "bosses lose nothing on their share options when share prices fall, but stand to make virtually unlimited gains if they rise". This is a sentiment echoed in the *Financial Times* (February 13, 1995): "In effect, option schemes are the original one-way bet. If the shares go down, the directors merely lose a potential profit opportunity. In contrast, shareholders incur genuine losses", and, later when commenting on the moves by Deutsche Bank and Daimler-Benz to offer share options to their top executives, the *Financial Times* (May 8, 1997) again commented "The terms offer management a one-way bet".

Some of these concerns are misplaced. While a grant of executive share options does indeed have value, even at the point of issue and even when the strike price equals the prevailing market price, if the value of the option grant is seen as part of the overall executive remuneration package then this should be seen as a form of deferred compensation, i.e. paid for up-front by the executive. In common with some other forms of deferred compensation, the final value will depend, among other things, on the performance of the executive in the job. The lack of explicit valuation (let alone recognition) of the option package when granted makes it easy to overlook this perspective. Thus, if one takes a typical CEO from a FTSE-100 company to have a level of base pay of £472,000 (the 1995 level) and assuming a 3% dividend yield, a 5% annual risk-free interest rate, a share price volatility of 0.33, and an option holding period of some 4 years, then the four times emoluments rule offers a total options package with a Black-Scholes valuation of £484,000. Given that the present value of 4 years of base pay in this situation is £1.76 m, then the options package represents an additional 28% of pay. If this is viewed as foregone cash pay, or deferred compensation, then a subsequent decline in share price will manifest itself in an ever decreasing valuation of the option package. This diminution of the wealth position is as potent a signal or incentive as a diminution that would arise out of a holding of company shares.

Indeed, it is possible to argue that it is a far more potent signal. It is true that the value of a share option moves less than proportionately with the underlying share price (approaching a one-for-one movement only when the option is very clearly 'in the money'), but this is more than compensated by the increased leverage offered by options. The leverage arises through the executive being able to purchase, out of a given amount of deferred compensation, options over a greater number of shares than it would be possible to own directly. This point is made in Figure 3 where the value of £472,000 worth of options is contrasted with the value of £472,000 worth of shares under two different performance outcomes. In Figure 3a share prices are assumed to decrease at 10% per year over the 4 year holding period, while in Figure 3b a 10% increase is assumed. Note that the usual chestnut about there being no downside risk with options is simply incorrect. For the same foregone pay, with rising share prices options bring more reward, and with falling share prices options bring more pain. Even the poorest of company performances leaves the executive's share holding with some residual value, but the entire value of the options package can easily be wiped out by a poor performance. This is a point to which we shall return in some detail below.

It is worth remembering in this context that Greenbury (1995: 6.28) claims that the traditional forms of executive share options "have drawbacks" because they bring "windfall gains" and do not lead the executive to "build up a substantial shareholding in their companies". This sentiment is echoed by the ABI (1994: 2) which recommends in terms of annual bonus payments that "some incentive should be given for part of the annual bonus payment to be

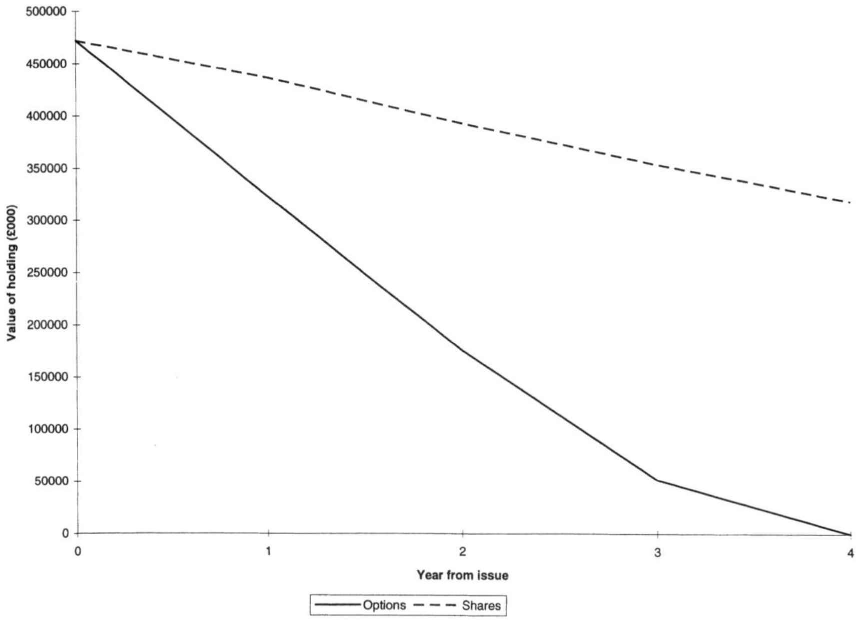

Figure 3a. Options vs. shares (–10% per annum share price growth)

invested in company shares to be held for three years or more". And in promoting long-term incentive schemes, Greenbury (1995, 6.32) argues that "schemes along these lines may be as effective, or more so, than improved share option schemes in linking rewards to performance". As reported above, arguments such as these have lead to the widespread move away from share options towards more share-based modes of compensation.

The improved share option schemes referred to by Greenbury are option schemes that place performance hurdles on exercise and/or issue of options. This is essentially a form of the super option which under ABI guidelines allowed an extra four time emoluments of options to be granted subject to a 5-year vesting period and a top-quartile of the FTSE-100 performance outcome for EPS. These arrangements simply increase the risk held by the executive (or the leverage of performance to reward). In the super options case it made them relatively unattractive. It could be argued that plain unadorned share options, if purchased by the executive by deferring current compensation, offer sufficient incentive and that the volume, or number, of option holdings offers a better adjustment mechanism for the compensation committee to use than the innate risk of a fixed holding of options through the manipulation of performance hurdles. Equally, any performance hurdles that are imposed on share holdings through Ltips can as easily be introduced to option packages.

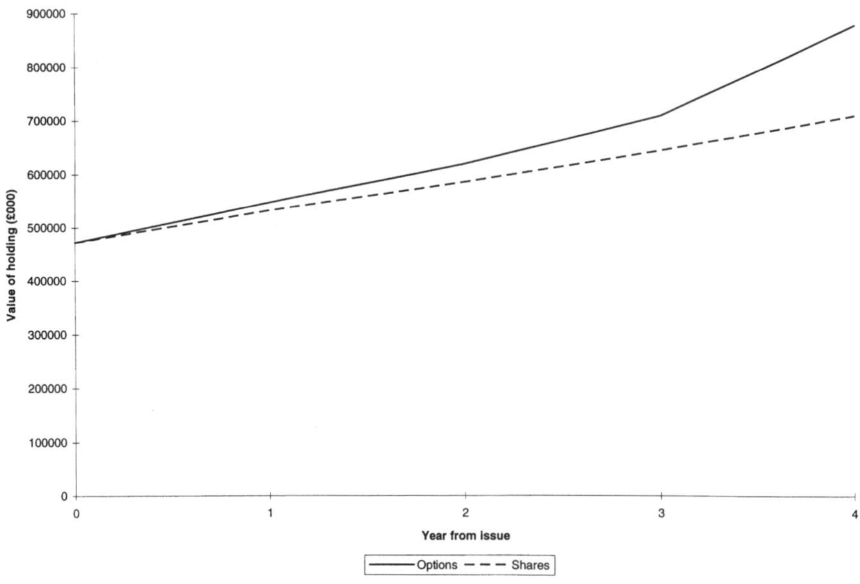

Figure 3b. Options vs. shares (+10% per annum share price growth)

Long term incentive plans (Ltips)

Following Pett (1996) it is possible to offer the following definition of an Ltip:

- A deferred right to receive shares at a nominal price or cost.
- The number of shares under such a scheme may be contingent upon company performance over a period of 3 years or so.
- There may be a requirement to hold shares once 'earned' for a further 2–3 years through a restriction on the right to dispose of the shares.
- At the end of any such restricted period the executive gets the full value of the shares and is liable to tax on that value.

Several variations of Ltips are possible. The most common in the UK is the performance share plan. This has a conditional award of shares allocated to the executive at zero cost. The number of shares awarded is conditional on the attainment of certain performance targets (sometimes relative to other companies) over a number of years, e.g. 3 years. Even when awarded, the shares generally do not vest until the passage of a further period after the actual performance period (2 years being typical). The award of shares is often expressed in terms of the executive's base salary, and the award will not generally be all or nothing but will taper from zero at a lower trigger point up to 100% at some defined upper performance standard. A 'performance equity plan', on the other hand, requires that executives invest at least part of what would normally be regarded as their cash bonus in company shares for a period of time (usually around 2 years) before the shares vest. An alternative arrangement is the unconditional share plan, which is akin to restricted share awards in the USA, with the executive merely having to remain with the company throughout the restriction period, after which the defined number of shares vest. These are rare in the UK (TeleWest being an exception) as they run contrary to the Greenbury Code.

The growing popularity of Ltips in Britain owes much to the relatively negative stance to option schemes taken by the Greenbury Committee, and the encouragement given therein to consideration of alternative forms of long-term incentive. Table 2, based on information provided in a report by New Bridge Street Consultants (1996), documents the decrease in popularity in share option schemes. Only 80% of companies report operating them for senior executives and 16% of these (e.g. BP) exclude executives who are subject to Ltips. Thus, option coverage could be as low as 64% at the top of large UK companies. This contrasts with the near universality found in the early 1990s by Towers Perrin (see Figure 1). Table 2(ii) also makes clear that most FTSE-100 companies are now imposing performance conditions on any executive share option schemes that they do operate. Of the 40 companies that have recently renewed their executive share option schemes, 83% have a clearly disclosed performance conditions, and only 5% have no condition attached. Earnings

Table 2. FTSE-100 use of executive share options and Ltips – August 1996

(i)	Executive share options:	
	Characteristic:	Percentage:
	Scheme in place?	
	Yes	80
	(Yes but not for Ltip participants)	16
	No	15
	Unknown	5
(ii)	Performance conditions on share option schemes: (for the 40 companies renewing their option scheme after July 1993)	
	Characteristic (%):	
	Condition disclosed	83
	No condition	5
	Condition not disclosed	7
	Not known	5
	Condition type* if disclosed (%):	
	Earnings per share	74
	Share price	12
	Shareholder return	24
	Other	6
	(*may sum to >100 as some schemes use more than one condition)	
(iii)	Long-term performance scheme (Ltip):	
	With Ltip (%):	58
	Number of plans**	64
	Performance share plan	48
	Performance equity plan	4
	Unconditional share plan	1
	Phantom share option	5
	Cash plan	6
	No Ltip:	43
	(**plan type may sum to more than number with plan as some companies may have more than one plan)	
(iv)	Performance share plans – type of performance measured (%)†:	
	Earnings per share	17
	Share price	4
	Shareholders return	75
	Other	10
	Unknown	6
	(†may sum to more than 100 as plans may utilize more than one measure, n=48 plans)	

(v) Benchmark (%) for various Ltip performance measures:

Benchmark	Performance measure§ EPS	Share price	Shareholder return
Index	–	50	58
Sector	–	–	8
Chosen group	–	–	38
Retail price index	50	50	–
% Growth rate	50	–	–
Unknown	–	–	3

(§may add to more than 100 as performance measures may utilize more than one benchmark)

(vi) Time horizon (%) over which performance is measured:

<3 years	0
3 years	71
4 years	17
5 years	2
>5 years	0
Unknown	10

Source: Abstracted from report by New Bridge Street Consultants (1996). Data as of 31 August 1996.

per share remains the most popular condition in this type of award.

In the survey results presented in Table 2(iii), a large proportion of companies, 58%, utilize Ltips. Of the Ltip schemes, the majority (52 of 64 schemes in the 58 companies) are of the performance share plan type, with most relying on shareholder return as a performance measure. It is also common (indeed almost universal) to gauge shareholder return not in absolute terms but against an index, or against some sector, or against some grouping of comparator companies. In general, 3 years is the typical performance period, but a few schemes extend to 4 years.

This all represents a fairly dramatic change from the early 1990s. There is a clear, and probably growing, move away from executive share options towards long-term incentive plans that incorporate performance measures over a 3 or 4 year period. These schemes reward in shares and often impose additional restrictions in terms of holding periods before the shares can be sold. We now attempt to examine the empirical impact on the pay–performance relationship of moving away from option-based schemes towards share-based schemes.

An empirical illustration

In an attempt to quantify the relative impact of executive share option plans and share-based Ltips, we utilize a sample of some 62 large British companies (see Appendix Table A1 for a list of the companies) between 1979 and 1997. These are FTSE-100 companies in 1997 and may, therefore, be atypical. In addition, as they have been traded continuously between 1979 and 1997, they are also by definition survivors. For the same reason they exclude the many privatizations that have occurred over the past decade or so. These various sample selection considerations may impart a bias, but our purpose is a simple one: to compare the pay–performance responsiveness of two stereotypical types of remuneration package.

Under one stereotype, it is assumed that the executive is issued with executive share options on an annual basis, with the value of the shares under option in each annual tranche equal to the value of the executive's base pay that year. The executive is assumed to hold the options for 4 years and then exercise the options and sell the resulting shares. This, then, approximates the ABI guideline as in steady state executives are holding options equal to four times their emoluments. The issuing of the options steadily over the period is in accord with the Greenbury recommendation that option grants be phased rather than issued in one large block. It also makes the calculations less arbitrarily dependent on timing.

The impact of company performance on the economic well-being of the executive will depend on how it affects the value of four distinct vintages of options. Thus the incentive effect of this variable component of pay will come from the value of the new options that are issued (that year's tranche of options), plus, more importantly, the change of value experienced over the year in each of the earlier vintages of options that are being held (i.e. the change over the latest year in the value of the options that were issued last year, plus the change over the same year in those issued 2 years ago, and so on). For the oldest vintage of options the asset would actually be realized (option exercised and shares sold) in cash terms.

By way of comparison, the other stereotype of remuneration package allows the executives to be granted, on an annual basis, shares to a value of their current level of base pay. It is assumed that sale or vesting of these shares is restricted for 4 years, after which time the executive duly sells the shares. In steady state the executive will be holding shares of value approximately four times base pay and from four distinct vintages, and will at year end be rewarded for performance in that year by an issue of new shares and the change in value on each of the four vintages of shares held (the oldest of which is assumed to be sold at that point).

The overall set-up is shown in Figure 4. Thus, for the companies in the sample, not until 1983 is there enough data to compute the total impact of a year's company performance on the variable component of pay enjoyed by the executive. From 1983 onwards it can be seen that in addition to the issue of a new tranche of options or share (V_0), there are also increases or decrease in value being realized on last year's issue (V_1–V_0), on the issue from 2 years ago (V_2–V_1), on the issue from 3 years ago (V_3–V_2), and from the 4 year old vintage (V_4–V_3). This oldest vintage is assumed to be sold at this point, but this transaction has no further impact as all changes in value that have occurred to the vintage since its issue have already been attributed to the year in which they occurred. Throughout this approach, therefore, we are assuming that, as far as incentive effects are concerned, putative (or paper) gains are regarded by the executive as if they are real. This undoubtedly exaggerates the effect, as any share price movement may be reversed before a particular vintage of option or share vests. But there is no double counting as only the increase (or decrease) in the value of the asset over the previous year is attributed at any one year end.

Measuring the increase in value of the options and shares held in the two plans is straightforward. Use is made of the London Business School's Risk Measurement Services Data Archive which provides monthly share prices and rates of return for all shares on the London Stock Exchange from March 1979 onwards. Care has to be taken to allow for capitalizations so that the correct share unit is used for each of the vintages of shares or options once issued.[2] For each of the 62 companies in the sample, the relevant annual report for 1995 was

[2] The London Share Price data tapes (London Business School) and Extel's Capital Gains Tax Service (1997) provide the necessary information regarding capitalizations so that the necessary adjustments are made in order to allow meaningful comparisons of share prices across time. For a few companies in the sample there was also the added complication of demerger. In each case it is assumed that the proceeds of the demerger (market value of the new company's shares on flotation day) are immediately reinvested in the focal company. Notable cases where this has occurred are: (i) Hanson (June 1, 1995 US Industries; October 1, 1996, Imperial Tobacco Group and Millenium Common; February 24, 1997 Energy Group). (ii) ICI (June 1, 1993 Zeneca). (iii) EMI (August 19, 1996 Thorn).

Vintage or year of issue	Year in which performance effects value. 79	80	81	82	83	84	85	86	87	88	89	90	91	92	93	94	95	96	97
79	V_0	V_1-V_0	V_2-V_1	V_3-V_2	V_4-V_3														
80		V_0	V_1-V_0	V_2-V_1	V_3-V_2	V_4-V_3													
81			V_0	V_1-V_0	V_2-V_1	V_3-V_2	V_4-V_3												
82				V_0	V_1-V_0	V_2-V_1	V_3-V_2	V_4-V_3											
83					V_0	V_1-V_0	V_2-V_1	V_3-V_2	V_4-V_3										
84						V_0	V_1-V_0	V_2-V_1	V_3-V_2	V_4-V_3									
85							V_0	V_1-V_0	V_2-V_1	V_3-V_2	V_4-V_3								
86								V_0	V_1-V_0	V_2-V_1	V_3-V_2	V_4-V_3							
87									V_0	V_1-V_0	V_2-V_1	V_3-V_2	V_4-V_3						
88										V_0	V_1-V_0	V_2-V_1	V_3-V_2	V_4-V_3					
89											V_0	V_1-V_0	V_2-V_1	V_3-V_2	V_4-V_3				
90												V_0	V_1-V_0	V_2-V_1	V_3-V_2	V_4-V_3			
91													V_0	V_1-V_0	V_2-V_1	V_3-V_2	V_4-V_3		
92														V_0	V_1-V_0	V_2-V_1	V_3-V_2	V_4-V_3	
93															V_0	V_1-V_0	V_2-V_1	V_3-V_2	V_4-V_3
94																V_0	V_1-V_0	V_2-V_1	V_3-V_2
95																	V_0	V_1-V_0	V_2-V_1
96																		V_0	V_1-V_0
97																			V_0

Figure 4. Description of data analysis

consulted and the base pay of the CEO was obtained. The retail price index was used to express this in the appropriate contemporaneous £ value. Referring to the prevailing share price then allows the number of shares or options to be issued in that period to be calculated. Although most expressions of the incentive effect of pay structure used below are in proportional terms, the use of the 1995 standard of base pay is a simplification that should be borne in mind (pre-1995 it was not always possible to separate base and bonus payments in published figures).

Once the number of shares or options issued in each year is known it is, therefore, a simple matter to follow each vintage over the 4 years of its life and to calculate the fluctuations in its value. For the options, an annual valuation of each of the outstanding vintages of options is taken by utilizing the latest share price, the latest annual dividend yield and the latest measure of variability along with the recorded strike price pertinent to that vintage of option to compute the option value according to the Black-Scholes-Merton formula.[3]

For each year it is therefore possible to compute the variable element of pay that arises through the change in value of option (or share) holdings. In any year, then, the incentive element of pay owes to the issue of new assets and the change in value of four vintages of assets already issued. This variable component can be expressed as a percentage of the base level of pay. In an attempt to estimate the strength of association between pay and performance under each of the two stereotypical pay schemes (option-based vs. share-based) the percentage of variable to base pay is regressed on total shareholder return

[3] In using the Black-Scholes-Merton formula the current divident yield, share price and volatility are available in the Risk Measurement Service Data Archive. All options are assumed to have a 4 year effective term at the outset and for each vintage this is reduced every year. The risk free rate used to evaluate the options is the annual yield on short-dated (5-year) government stock for that year. This is available in *Financial Statistics*.

in that year. Fractions rather than logarithms are used here as it is quite possible, in the face of a share price collapse, that the variable component of pay is negative.

In a rather simplistic way, then, we can estimate the pay–performance correlation across this sample of 62 companies and 15 years (1983–1997). Table 3 displays the results. Reflecting the panel nature of the data, a two factor-model allowing for company-specific and time-specific effects is estimated. In comparing part (i) and part (ii) of this table, it seems that there is very little difference between option-based and share-based incentive schemes.[4] In both cases there is a highly significant relationship between pay and performance. This is not unexpected as there is a close if not definitional relationship between the dependent and descriptive variables. In the case of shares, a company's dividend policy can disturb the relationship.[5] In the case of options, the relationship is not definitional because there is not only the matter of dividends, which increase shareholder return but not option value, but also

Table 3. Regression results for optimum vs. shares stimulation (dependent variable is variable pay realized that year as a fraction of base pay). With company-specific and time-specific fixed effects.

Descriptive variable	*Est. coefficient*	*(t-statistic)**
(i) Options: (1xbase pay exercise value of shares under option issued each year)		
Shareholder return	3.802	(41.54)
R-squared	0.75	
F-statistic (prob. value)	36.86	(0.00)
Chi-squared on fixed effects (prob. value)	213.94	(0.00)
(ii) Shares (1xbase pay worth of shares issued each year)		
Shareholder return	4.216	(47.51)
R-squared	0.79	
F-statistic (prob. value)	47.06	(0.00)
Chi-squared on fixed effects (prob. value)	171.74	(0.00)
(iii) Options: (1xbase pay worth of options issued each year – same monetary value as (ii))		
Shareholder return	14.312	(38.45)
R-squared	0.72	
F-statistic (prob. value)	31.72	(0.00)
Chi-squared on fixed effects (prob. value)	197.15	(0.00)

*White heteroskedastic corrected covariance matrix used.

4 The hypothesis that the coefficients on shareholder return in Table 3(i) and Table 3(ii) are equal (specifically that the coefficient in the option regression equals 4.216) is rejected with a *t*-statistic of 4.526.

5 It is assumed that the shares do not pay dividends while subject to restrictions.

the matter of share options that are under water or only close to the strike price. In these cases there is nothing like the one-for-one relationship between share return and option value. Nevertheless the result seems clear: there is a close and empirically strong relationship between company performance and executive pay in both of these approaches.

Dimensionally the relationship is around 4.0. This suggests that for a 1% change in shareholder return then executive pay rises by 4% of base pay. Of course, with large companies of the type under consideration here, a 1% increase in shareholder return may be worth many £millions. For example, average market capitalization in the sample was £5,276 m in 1995 and average base pay was £472,000. Thus for a £52.76 m increase in shareholder wealth the executive is rewarded by some £18,880. This falls far short of what principal-agent theory might suggest as desirable, while representing a stronger relationship than is found for the real world in many empirical studies (e.g. Jensen and Murphy, 1990a,b).

One important difference between share-based and option-based incentive plans emerges when one considers the value of the assets issued to the executives under these alternative programmes. In the case of options the typical executive receives an annual allocation of options that at issue are of value £96,812. This may be measured against the sample average level of base pay in this exercise of £384,759. In the case of shares the value at issue has an annual average of £384,759 (by construction equal to the annual base pay). This is because by definition the executive receives the equivalent of his/her base pay in shares each year. In the case of options what is received is an allocation of options over shares with that face value. The value of an option on a share is considerably less than the strike price or value of the share at the point of issue – due to the risk over the life of the option (assumed to be 4 years here). The executive absorbs that risk, hence the lower cost to the company.

An alternative way to view the situation is to investigate the pay–performance sensitivity of an executive share option plan where options are issued to a value equal to that of the share-based package (i.e. with option value measured by our crude Black-Scholes approximation to the fair market value, which is in reality not, of course, readily ascertainable). We therefore ask what the pay–performance relationship would be if companies annually issued CEOs a tranche of options with approximate market value equal to their base salary?

To answer this question, Table 3(iii) recomputes the variable component of pay if options of market value (according to the Black-Scholes-Merton formula) equal to base pay are issued, i.e. averaging £384,759 across the sample. Numerically, this allows almost four time more shares under option to be issued, and results in a much stronger pay–performance relationship. The estimated coefficient rises from 3.802 to 14.312. In terms of value for money to the company share options are a better deal, but, of course, we are not comparing like with like, as to the executive the share option package is much riskier. But the comparison is none the less illuminating in terms of exposing the potency of executive share options.

Table 4. Regression results from options vs shares stimulation (dependent variable is variable pay realized that year as a fraction of base pay). With company-specific and time-specific fixed effects.

Descriptive variable	*Est. coefficient (t-statistic)**	
(i) Options: (1 × base pay exercise value of shares under option issued each year)		
Shareholder return:		
return-p	3.938	(37.75)
return-n	2.752	(6.83)
R-squared	0.75	
F-statistic (prob. value)	36.74	(0.00)
Chi-squared on fixed effects (prob. value)	205.33	(0.00)
(ii) Shares (1 × base pay worth of shares issued each year)		
Shareholder return:		
return-p	4.150	(40.91)
return-n	4.720	(12.05)
R-squared	0.79	
F-statistic (prob. value)	46.52	(0.00)
Chi-squared on fixed effects (prob. value)	173.64	(0.00)
(iii) Options: (1 × base pay worth of options issued each year – same monetary value as (ii))		
Shareholder return:		
return-p	15.131	(35.85)
return-n	7.964	(4.89)
R-squared	0.72	
F-statistic (prob. value)	32.06	(0.00)
Chi-squared on fixed effects (prob. value)	198.17	(0.00)

*White heteroskedastic corrected covariance matrix used.

The current framework may also be extended to examine the 'lack of downside' claim that is frequently made regarding executive share options. The analysis in Table 3 is repeated, but with the descriptive variable being split into two parts. In one, return-p, we enter the shareholder return for that company and year where it is positive, but set the variable to zero otherwise. In the second descriptive variable, return-n, we enter shareholder return where it is zero or negative, but set the variable to zero if it is positive. This decomposition allows us to measure any asymmetry in the responsiveness of the incentive pay package to an upwards versus a downwards movement in shareholder wealth. It is clear from inspection of the results in Table 4(ii) that with a share-based incentive plan the responsiveness of pay to performance is much more symmetrical (in fact exactly symmetrical[6]). With option-based

[6] It is not possible to reject the hypothesis that in Table 4(ii) $B_{return\text{-}p}=B_{return\text{-}n}=4.216$ (as in Table 3(ii)), with *t*-statistics of 0.65 and 1.29 respectively.

plans, described in Table 4(i), there is, indeed, a difference in reaction with executives suffering less for falls in shareholder wealth than they are rewarded for increases in shareholder wealth. It is important to note that, contrary to the claims of many commentators the responsiveness of executive pay under option-based schemes is very significantly (both statistically and empirically) different from zero. It is clear that, on average, executives are carrying options of sufficient 'market value' at any time to expose them to a significant downside risk were company returns to turn negative.

When the expense of the option plan to the company is allowed to equal the expense of the share plan, as shown in Table 4(iii), the asymmetry remains as before but the empirical size of the coefficients becomes interesting. At 7.964 the response in an option-based plan is around half the 15.131 obtaining in the face of positive returns, but in terms of value for money, the same cost to the company produces a pay–performance sensitivity with a negative shareholder return of only 4.720 under share plans (Table 4(ii)) as opposed to 7.964 under option-plans. This is a statistically and empirically significant difference. Options seem to come out ahead. This suggests that the increased leverage available in terms of option-based incentive schemes can outweigh this dulling of the downward responsiveness.

In considering these results, it is important to consider some of the weaknesses of the assumptions made in deriving them. One weakness is that the study focuses on the company as the unit of analysis rather than the individual. If the same person was CEO during the entire period then this would make no difference, but given that a new CEO may arrive in post with less than our assumed holdings of options or shares of various vintages, then we will be overestimating the pay–performance sensitivity. These results are certainly much stronger than obtained by Main *et al.* (1996) in an examination of actual boardroom holdings of executive share options in the UK. Empirically, however, the impact of any bias here will be symmetrical, in the sense that comparison between the power of option-based and share-based plans remains approximately correct.

Furthermore, no attempt has been made to introduce performance conditions. Both the option-based and share-based incentive schemes modeled above are assumed to vest without further restriction or qualification at the end of the 4 year holding period. Given the strictures of the Greenbury Report in terms of adding performance hurdles to both executive share options and Ltips, this may seem to be a major drawback. However, while adding performance hurdles would increase the pay-performance responsiveness, it could be argued that this would occur to no greater extent in one type of scheme vs. the other. Again, we would argue that the relative comparison remains valid.

The conclusion seems to remain, therefore, that the use of options in preference to shares allows a given pay–performance relationship to be attained much less expensively (to the company). Alternatively, for the same cost options can produce a much higher pay–performance relationship than share based schemes. It would appear, therefore, that the move away from using executive share options towards using share-based payment schemes may be an expensive one for companies and shareholders.

An additional consideration is the complexity that comes with Ltip schemes. This arises in terms of design: which performance hurdles? which comparator groups? It also arises in terms of implementation: were the conditions met? to what extent? All of this opens the door for discretion and bias in decision making. The fact that the type of social processes that cause biases in most realms of human decision making are also at work in the boardroom in the process of CEO pay determination has been documented by O'Reilly *et al.* (1988), Main *et al.* (1993, 1995) and others. For example, in a recent annual report (February, 1997) British Aerospace describe their new Ltip and claim that the Nomination and Compensation Committee uses two performance criteria, total shareholder return (TSR) and earnings per share excluding exceptional items. They point out that "Both the TSR and EPS performance measures may be adjusted for exceptional items as appropriate at the discretion of the Committee". Thus when computing executive entitlements, one can see the scope for discretion. Equally, when some companies retain the facility to vary during the course of the Ltip the comparator companies against which performance is being measured, one again is reminded of the scope for discretion.

Executive share option schemes, if clearly costed and implemented in a way which makes them a deferred compensation component of the executive's overall compensation package, have some very attractive features in terms of linking pay and performance. Ltips may be easier to explain to shareholders and they may offer the remuneration committee a greater sense of control, but as an alternative they seem to be relatively expensive and much more prone to slippage in the implementation stage than option-based incentive schemes.

Summary and policy implications

Executive share options in Britain, and to a much lesser extent in the rest of Europe, have enjoyed a very bad press over recent years. Due to a combination of tax incentives provided in the British 1984 statutory scheme and a general move towards incentive based pay, executive share options came into widespread use throughout British boardrooms. Remuneration committees failed to ensure, however, that the share option package was clearly valued and seen to be an integral part of overall remuneration (a deferred component bought by the employee by way of lower current compensation). This failure means that many commentators, rightly or wrongly, see the share option package as icing on the cake or an add-on to what is viewed as already highly generous levels of pay.

The handling of newly privatized companies in Britain (particularly the utilities) was especially unfortunate in this regard. In many of these cases, initial executive option packages were granted at flotation prices when such prices turned out to be well below the subsequent traded market price. In other cases, the press highlighted instances of significant gains from options while failing to clarify that such gains are based on a lengthy period of performance, of the order of 4 years in general. Situations where option packages fail to yield any gains are not usually publicized.

In the UK, the mounting outcry led the Greenbury Committee to give a clear steer away from option packages towards other forms of long-term remuneration. Anxious as ever to comply with official (and semi-official) codes of practice, many companies have already taken significant steps towards abandoning executive share option packages and instituting what are commonly labeled Ltips or long-term incentive plans. These are usually share based and echo the restricted stock plans once common in the USA, although generally involving well defined performance hurdles.

The empirical illustration presented above argues that such moves are generally unnecessary and ill advised. Ltips involve a substantial amount of discretion on the part of remuneration committees as to which performance criteria are to be chosen, how these criteria are to be judged to have been met, and so on. It is now well established that there are very strong social forces at play in a board room, and that these forces can easily influence non-executive directors into making executive pay awards that are more generous than would have been expected based on the fundamentals of the situation.

It is argued here, partly by empirical illustration, that executive share options remain a highly potent form of remuneration in terms of value for money in linking pay to performance. In terms of the implementation of an option-based remuneration policy, the key seems to be first to determine the average level of remuneration that the company feels necessary to attract and retain the executive in question, and then to persuade the executive to take as large a proportion of such remuneration in the form of share options as is appropriate to the executive and to the company's desire for a pay-performance linkage. This will require an explicit valuation of the worth of executive share options at the time of issue.

Reliance on share options has the virtue of being transparent, relatively free from arbitrary board level judgments, and cheap. It also pays the executive in a way that the general shareholder can, if it looks such a good idea, invest in. Whereas the usual Ltip is beyond the access of most individuals, a purchase of share options, at least in the larger companies, and admittedly for a shorter term, is something we can all engage in.

In many ways, the well intentioned Greenbury Committee has given an unfortunate steer away from option-based incentive schemes and towards Ltips. To date the Hampel Committee has failed to reverse this. There is mounting evidence that UK companies are energetically implementing Ltip schemes and abandoning option schemes. It would be a pity if such a cost effective, objective, and relatively transparent incentive device as executive share options were to be abandoned in favor of such a cumbersome, expensive, and opaque replacement.

Table A1. List of companies utilized, 1979–1997.

Number	*Company name*	*Number*	*Company*
1	Allied Domecq	32	Lloyds TSB
2	ASD	33	Marks & Spencer
3	Assoc. Brit Foods	34	MEPC
4	Bank of Scotland	35	Natwest Bank
5	Barclays	36	P&O
6	Bass	37	Prudential
7	BAT Indus	38	Rank Group
8	Blue Circle	39	Reckitt & Coleman
9	BOC	40	Reed Int'l
10	Boots	41	Rentokil Initial
11	BP	42	REXAM
12	Burton	43	RMC
13	Cad Schweppes	44	RTZ
14	Comm Union	45	Sainsbury
15	DE LARUE	46	Schroders
16	Dixons	47	Scottish & Newcastle
17	EMI	48	SEARS
18	Gen Accident	49	Shell Transport
19	General Electric	50	Siebe
20	GKN	51	Smith & Nephew
21	Glaxo Wellcome	52	Smiths Indus.
22	Granada	53	SmKl Beecham
23	Grand Met	54	Standard Chtrd
24	Guinness	55	Tate & Lyle
25	GUS	56	Tesco
26	Hanson	57	TI Group
27	ICI	58	Tomkins
28	INCHCAPE	59	Unilever
29	Kingfisher	60	United News and Media
30	Ladbroke	61	Whitbread
31	Legal & General	62	Wolseley

References

Accounting Standards Board (1994) *Disclosure of Directors' Share Options*. Urgent Issues Task Force, Information Sheet No.11, London.

Association of British Insurers (1995). *Share Option and Profit Sharing Incentive Schemes*. ABI, London.

Association of British Insurers (1994). *Long Term Remuneration for Senior Executives*. ABI, London.

Association of British Insurers (1993). *Share Scheme Guidance. A Joint Statement from the Investment Committees of the ABI and NAPF.* ABI, London.

Association of British Insurers (1991). *Share Incentive Scheme Guidelines. Memorandum*. ABI, London.

Bey, R.P. and L.J. Johnson (1994). *Valuation of Executive Stock Options*. College of Business Administration, University of Tulsa.

Black, F. and M. Scholes (1973). The pricing of options and corporate liabilities. *Journal of Political Economy*, **81**, 637–654.

Cadbury Committee (1992). *The Financial Aspects of Corporate Governance*. Professional Publishing Ltd., London.

Conyon, M., P. Gregg and S. Machin (1995). Taking care of business: executive compensation in the UK. *Economic Journal*, **105**, 704–714.

Cox, J., S. Ross and M. Rubinstein (1979). Option pricing: a simplified approach. *Journal of Financial Economics*, **7**, 229–263.

Cuny, C.J. and P. Jorion (1995). Valuing executive share options with endogenous departure. *Journal of Accounting and Economics*, **20**, 193–205.

European Union (1992). *Promotion of Participation by Employed Persons in Profit and Enterprise Results*. PEPPER Report. Recommendation of the Council of the EU, 27 July, 92/443/EEC.

Financial Accounting Standards Board (1993). *Accounting for Stock-Based Compensation*. FASB, Hartford, Connecticut.

Financial Accounting Standards Board (1994). *FASB Agrees Not to Require Expense Recognition for Stock Options*. FASB, Hartford, Connecticut.

Foster, T.W., P.R. Koogler and D. Vickrey (1991). Valuation of executive stock options and the FASB proposal. *The Accounting Review*, **66**, 595–610.

Foster, T.W., P.R. Koogler and D. Vickrey (1993). Valuation of executive stock options and the FASB proposal: an extension. *Accounting Review*, **68**, 184–189.

Greenbury, R. (1995). *Directors' Remuneration. Report of a Study Group Chaired by Sir Richard Greenbury*. Gee Publishing Ltd., London.

Hampel, R. (1997). *Committee on Corporate Governance. Preliminary Report*. London Stock Exchange.

Hemmer, T., S. Matsunga and T. Shevlin (1994). Estimating the 'fair value' of employee stock options with early exercise. *Accounting Horizons*, **8**, (December).

Hemmer, T., S. Matsunga and T. Shevlin (1996). The influence of risk diversification on the early exercise of employee stock options by executive officers. *Journal of Accounting and Economics*, **21**, 45–68.

Huddart, S. (1994). Employee stock options. *Journal of Accounting and Economics*, **18**, 207–231.

Huddart, S. and M. Lang (1996). Employee stock options. An empirical analysis. *Journal of Accounting and Economics*, **21**, 5–43.

Inland Revenue (1984). *Finance Act 1984. Approved Share Option Schemes. Explanatory Notes*. Inland Revenue, London.

Institutional Shareholders' Committee (1991). *The Responsibilities of Institutional Shareholders in the UK*. Institutional Shareholders' Committee, London.

Jennergren, L.P. and B. Naslund (1993). A comment on 'valuation of executive stock options and the FASB proposal'. *Accounting Review*, **68**, 179–183.

Jensen, M.C. and K.J. Murphy (1990a). Performance pay and top-management incentives. *Journal of Political Economy*, **98**, 225–264.

Jensen, M.C. and K.C. Murphy (1990b). CEO incentives – it's not how much you pay, but how. *Harvard Business Review*, **90**, 139–153.

Labour Party (1994). *Five New Share Millionaires*. News Release, 18 August. Labour Party, London.

London Stock Exchange (1995). *The Listing Rules (Yellow Book)*. London Stock Exchange, London.

Main, B., A. Bruce and T. Buck (1996). Total board remuneration and company performance. *Economic Journal*, **106**, 1627–1644.

Main, B.G.M., C.A. O'Reilly III and J. Wade (1993). Top executive pay: tournament or teamwork? *Journal of Labor Economics*, **11**, 606–628.

Main, B.G.M., C.A. O'Reilly and J. Wade (1995). The CEO, the board of directors, and executive compensation: economic and psychological perspectives. *Industrial and Corporate Change*, **4**, 293–332.

Merton, R.C. (1973). Theory of rational option pricing. *Bell Journal of Economics and Management Science*, **4**, 141–183.

Monks Partnership (1997). *Board Earnings in FT-SE 100 Companies*. Monks, Saffron Walden, Essex.

Monks Partnership (1996). *Remuneration of Directors and Managers – Europe*. Monks, Saffron Walden, Essex.

Mozes, H.A. (1994). *Accounting for the Firm's Cost of Employee Stock Options*, Fordham University, Graduate School of Business Administration.

National Association of Pension Funds (1992). *Share Schemes – A Consultative Approach*. NAPF, London.

National Association of Pension Funds (1984). *Share Schemes*, NAPF, London.

New Bridge Street Consultants (1996). *Paying for Performance. Long-term Incentives in the Top 500 UK Listed Companies*. New Bridge Street Consultants, London.

Noreen, E. and M. Wolfson (1981). Equilibrium warrant pricing models and accounting for executive stock options, *Journal of Accounting Research*, **19**, 384–398.

O'Reilly, C.A. III, B.G.M. Main and G.S. Crystal (1988). CEO compensation as tournament and social comparison: a tale of two theories. *Administrative Science Quarterly*, **33**, 257–274.

Pett, D. (1996). *Employee Share Schemes*. FT Law and Tax, Pearson Professional Ltd., London.

Robertson, Sir Lewis (1995). Corporate governance: the lessons of recent British experience. *Hume Papers on Public Policy*, **3**, 1–11.

Securities and Exchange Commission (1993). Securities Act Release No. 6962 and No. 7009. Securities and Exchange Commission, Washington, D.C.

Smith, C.W. and J.L. Zimmerman (1976). Valuing employee stock option plans using option pricing models, *Journal of Accounting Research*, **14**, 357–364.

Towers Perrin (1993). *Long Term Incentive Practice. Supplementary Report of Top Executive Remuneration*, Towers Perrin, London.

Vesley, H. and H. Shannon (1994). Income tax treatment of U.S. stock options plans in Europe. *Intertax*, **2**, 46–71.

Yermack, D. (1995). Do corporations award CEO stock options effectively? *Journal of Financial Economics*, **39**, 237–269.

STEVEN HUDDART
Duke University

8. Patterns of stock option exercise in the United States

Introduction

Stock options granted by an employer corporation to its employees offer many benefits. They:

(i) provide optionees with incentives to increase the stock price of the firm;

(ii) serve as 'golden handcuffs' that bind optionees to firms during the vesting period;

(iii) allow optionees to recognize income at times that coincide with favorable tax treatment or personal liquidity needs; and,

(iv) may be treated as 'off income statement compensation' by the employer for financial statement purposes.

Of course options also have costs. They:

(i) dilute existing shareholders' interests in the firm (but increase cash inflows to the firm);

(ii) expose optionees to the risk of fluctuations in the employer's stock price; and,

(iii) cause optionees to trade in their employer's stock and therefore put them at risk of violating insider trading rules.

Employee exercise behavior is essential to an understanding of both the benefits and costs of options. For instance, stock option grants often are intended to motivate employees to increase the employer's stock price. The beneficial incentives created by options depend on when and why employees exercise their options. In particular, the duration of the incentive differs if

---

I am grateful to Jack Hughes for helpful advice.

J. Carpenter and D. Yermack (eds.), Executive Compensation and Shareholder Value, 115–142.

employees exercise options for cash immediately on the vest date rather than holding them until expiration, especially since many options have 10 year lives but vest over 4 years. FAS 123 mandates disclosure of stock option compensation costs in corporate financial statements and the SEC requires that proxies state a value for the options granted to the five most highly compensated employees.[1] It is permissible to take exercise behavior into account in computing option costs for these external reporting purposes. Exercise behavior should also affect the computation of stock option costs that corporations undertake for internal decision making, such as setting compensation level and mix. Furthermore, an understanding of employee exercise behavior potentially influences the choice of exercise restrictions such as vesting provisions.

This chapter considers employee exercise behavior from three perspectives. In section 2, employee stock options (ESOs) are distinguished from traded stock options (TSOs) and certain valuation considerations peculiar to employee stock options are reviewed. Section 3 summarizes employee exercise behavior at a small sample of companies and relates this behavior to the valuation issues. Section 4 details the impact of taxation on employee exercise decisions and considers some tax planning opportunities afforded by options.

This paper is largely a synthesis of existing research. More detail on certain of the topics covered can be found in the references.

VALUATION

This section presents an analytical framework for exploring the valuation consequences of the features that distinguish employee stock options (ESOs) from traded stock options (TSOs). The framework includes the Black-Scholes formula as a special case. Numerical examples convey the importance of these features to the valuation of ESOs.

Characteristics of employee stock options

It is important to distinguish ESOs from TSOs. While the exercise of a TSO does not affect the welfare of holders of the underlying stock, the exercise of an ESO is dilutive since the corporation issues new stock to the optionee. Thus, ESOs are a type of warrant. While TSOs usually mature within one year of the date of issue, ESOs may be exercised in a window of time that extends over many years (see Figure 1). ESOs, in common with TSOs, are usually 'American' not 'European' options (i.e. they can be exercised any time during the exercise window, not just at maturity).[2]

---

[1] Many of these values are computed using the Black-Scholes formula, but FAS 123 and SEC regulation S-K §229.402 permit options to be valued using other option pricing models.

[2] After options vest, there are typically no restrictions on when they may be exercised, though corporate compensation committees may impose conditions on the exercise of ESOs, like attainment of specific accounting or performance targets, which do not apply to TSOs.

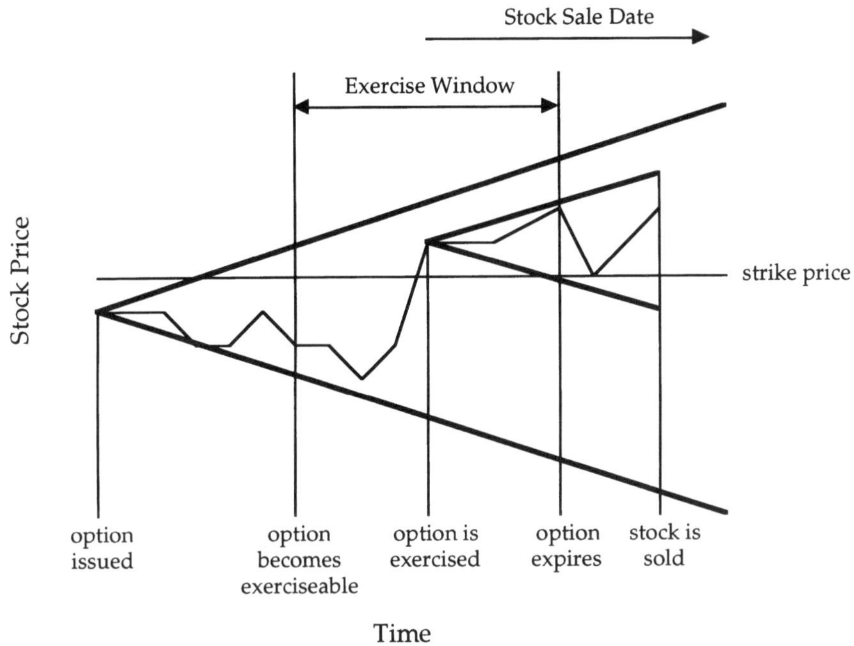

Figure 1. Nature of employee stock options. Employee stock options often are not exercisable for some years after issuance. The option may be exercised before expiration. The employee may sell the stock at any time after she exercises the option.

An important restriction on ESOs is that they cannot be sold by the employee to whom they are issued, and it is impractical for an employee to implement a trading strategy that would have the same effect as selling the option. Since ESOs cannot be traded, the pricing and optimal exercise policies for TSOs, which rely on the absence of arbitrage opportunities between the option and a portfolio that duplicates the return of the option do not apply to ESOs. Since the employee cannot trade freely in either the option or the underlying stock, the value of the option to the employee, the optimal exercise policy, and the cost to the employer do not follow the classical arguments in the option pricing literature. Factors like risk aversion and liquidity needs in imperfect capital markets complicate exercise behavior and make valuation more difficult.

It is straightforward to illustrate the importance of exercise behavior on the valuation of ESOs. The expected cost of the dilution suffered by the existing shareholders caused by granting the option depends on the employee's exercise policy. Suppose the employee's policy is to exercise the option only at maturity. For simplicity, consider an American option granted at the money on a stock paying no dividends. Then the Black-Scholes value approximates the expected cost of the dilution. Now suppose the employee's policy is to exercise the option on the first occasion it is in the money. Then the expected cost is nearly zero. In practice, the exercise policy of employees, and the expected cost to shareholders, lie somewhere between these extremes.

Ideally, shareholders want to know whether the benefits of options, in terms of retaining and motivating an employee, exceed the associated cost. This problem is exceedingly complex if the actions or trading strategies of the employees have an effect on the stock price, and strategies or actions differ depending on the employees' stake in the corporation. As a first step in attacking this challenging problem, assume stock price movements over time do not depend on employee actions. Where the employer grants stock options to low- and mid-level employee, it seems likely that the effect of any individual employee's action or exercise strategy on the stock price is negligible. Accordingly, the incentive effect of options for these employees should be small. Hence, the effect of granting options to low- and mid-level employees on the evolution of the stock price also should be small. Where the employer grants stock options to top executives, this assumption is less plausible. However, any increase in the cost of the option due to incentive effects is less than the concomitant expected increase in the value of the stock outstanding at the time the option is granted. Ignoring the incentive effect in valuing the option provides a benchmark cost that can be compared to alternate forms of compensation.

Binomial model

The binomial model of Cox *et al.* (1979) is the workbench for the intuitions presented in this section. Figure 2 depicts changes in stock price over time as an ingrown tree. At every node of the tree, the stock price moves up with probability p or down with probability $1\text{–}p$. On an uptick, the stock price increased by a factor of $s > 1$. On a downtick, the stock price falls by a factor of $1/s$. Thus, if the initial stock price is 1 and after i periods there have been k upticks (and $i - k$ downticks), the stock price in period i is s^j where $j = 2k - i$. Denote by (i,j) the node at time i in which the stock price is s^j. The number of steps in the tree, the probability of an uptick, and the factor by which the stock price increases on an uptick, can be chosen to approximate the distribution of future stock returns so that a probability can be assigned to each future stock price path. Option values may be computed as follows: determine when exercise takes place along each path and compute the difference between the stock price on the exercise date and the strike price. The sum over every path of these quantities, discounted to reflect time value and weighted by an appropriate probability measure, represents the expected present value of the option.

Any option valuation process must begin by specifying some parameters. The expiration date, vesting schedule, strike price and current stock price are readily determinable. Future interest rates, dividend yields, and stock volatilities are more difficult to determine. The most difficult estimates concern

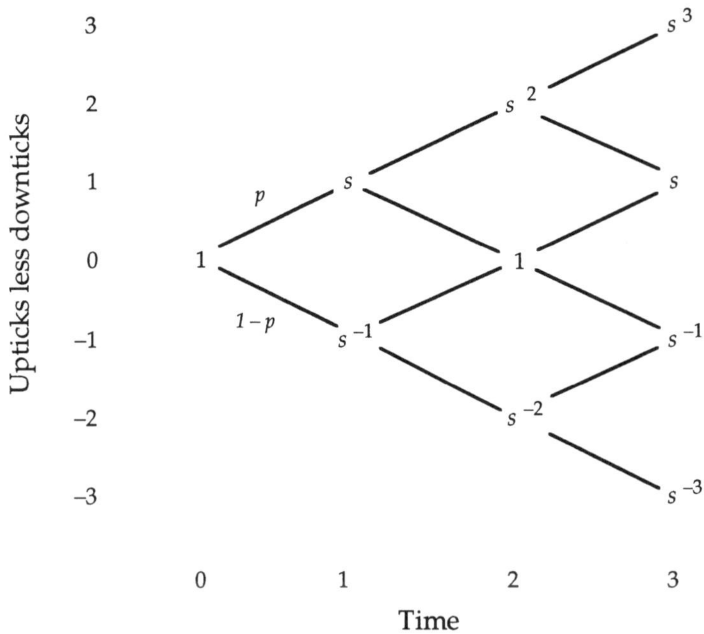

Figure 2. The binomial model of stock price evolution. An ingrown tree depicts stock price movements. At every node, the probability of an uptick is p. The probability of a downtick is $1-p$. On an uptick (downtick), the stock price increases (decreases) by a factor of s $(1/s)$.

employee exercise behavior. Reasons for exercise before expiration include employee risk aversion and liquidity needs, separation from the employer and dividend capture. The last of these has been thoroughly examined in the finance literature. Each of the other issues has been analyzed in a binomial framework (see, e.g. Carpenter, 1998; Cuny and Jorion, 1995; Huddart, 1994). To illustrate the general approach, I describe the impact of risk aversion in some detail.

Since an employee's total personal wealth (e.g. options, stock, salary and human capital) is typically concentrated in assets that are highly correlated with the employer's stock price, we may expect employees to exercise options in order to hold better diversified, less risky portfolios. The example below illustrates how the optimal option exercise policy depends on the risk aversion of the employee and how exercise before expiration may be optimal.

Consider the tree in Figure 2. At time zero, the employer grants the employee an option to buy stock at a strike price of $X = 1$ at either time 1, time 2, or time 3. Suppose the probability of an uptick is $p = \frac{2}{3}$ at every node. Following an uptick the stock price doubles (i.e. $s = 2$). After a downtick, the stock price falls by half. The expected return from holding the stock is equal to the expected return from holding the riskless asset, $ps + (1-p)/s = d$, so $d = 1.5$. To keep the analysis simple, assume no taxes are imposed on the optionee.

Suppose the employee evaluates exercise strategies according to the distribution of her wealth at the maturity of the option. If she exercises the option at node (2,2), she receives $(s^2 - 1)$ to be invested for one period at rate d. If she waits, she receives $(s^3 - 1)$ with a probability of p and $(s - 1)$ with a probability of $1 - p$. The employee will wait to exercise if she prefers the gamble of waiting to the payoff from exercising now. This relationship holds more generally. The employee will exercise the option at $(1, 1)$ if, and only if, $EU(d^2(s - 1)) > pEU[B(2, 2)] + (1 - p)EU[B(2, 0)]$ where $EU(\cdot)$ denotes expected utility for terminal wealth and $B(i, j)$ is the stochastic payment realized by the employee from carrying out the optimal strategy at (i, j).

A risk-neutral employee only exercises the option at nodes $(3, 3)$ and $(3, 1)$. When the employee has square root utility, she strictly prefers exercising the option at $(2, 2)$ to waiting until either $(3, 3)$ or $(3, 1)$ obtains. When the employee is more risk averse, she finds it optimal to exercise the option at $(1, 1)$ as well. Early exercise means paying the exercise price early. Acceleration of this payment reduces the risk of the final payoff by allowing the employee to switch from an investment in the risky option to a less risky asset, at the cost of lowering the expected return.

Optimal exercise policy

The optimal exercise policy for an ESO can be found from a recursive algorithm. The algorithm is a straightforward extension of the machinery used in the example. Figure 3 presents the optimal exercise policy in a specific case (using plausible parameter values) and gives the intuition for the regions of (time, stock price) space where exercise is optimal. The plot assumes the option vests 2 years after the date of grant. The set of nodes at which the employee chooses to exercise grows larger as the employee becomes more risk averse.

A risk-neutral employee never exercises the option early because the expected payoff from holding the option to maturity always exceeds the expected payoff from early exercise. Besides the expected payoff, a risk-averse employee also cares about the shape of the payoff distribution. The payoffs from exercising the option now or at maturity differ in this regard. The possible payoffs from holding the option to maturity resemble a standard lognormal distribution shifted left (by payment of the exercise price) and truncated at zero. The probability mass from the truncated section of the distribution is assigned to the zero payoff. Since there is a significant chance the option will expire out of the money, holding the option entails a large probability of a zero payoff. Exercising the option early to hold the stock offers a lower expected return, but there is no chance of a zero payoff. If the employee evaluates the payoff distribution from exercising the option now as sufficiently less risky than holding the option until the next period, she will exercise now. The reduction in risk compensates her for the lower expected payoff.

Suppose the employer grants the employee an option to buy 10,000 shares of the firm's stock that vest after 2 years and expire at the end of 5 years. Suppose

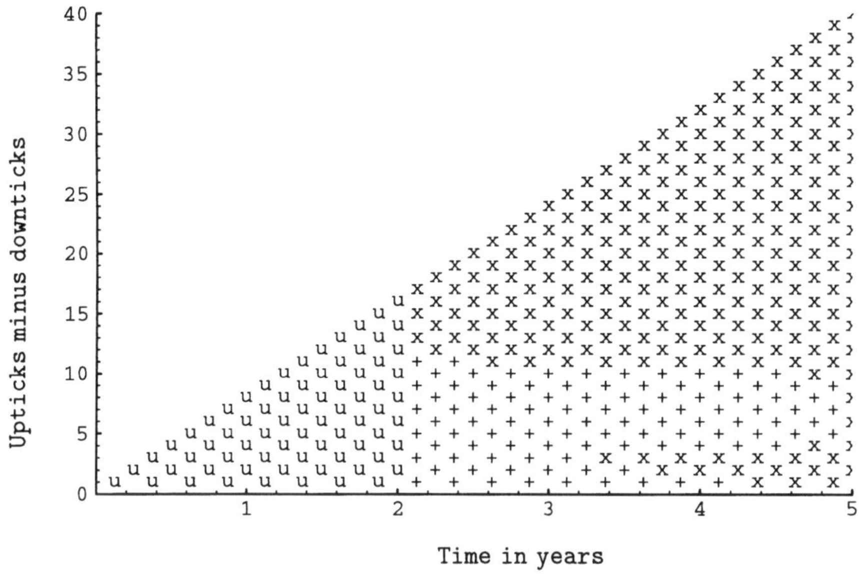

Figure 3. Graphical representations of optimal exercise policy. This figure plots the optimal exercise policy for an ESO that matures after 5 years and is owned by a risk averse employee. The employee is assumed to have a terminal utility for wealth give by $U(W) = W^{1/4}$. The option does not vest until two years after the grant date. A riskless asset offering the same expected return as the stock is available. The optimal policy in (time, stock price) space is shown by: x, exercise; u, the employee cannot exercise the option because it has not vested; +, hold the option until next period. A 40-step binomial model with parameters $p = 0.558926$ and $s = 1.1119$ approximates the evolution of the price of a stock with annual mean return of $\mu = 0.1$ and volatility of $\sigma = 0.3$.

further the initial stock price and the strike price are both \$20. Consistent with the parameters underlying Figure 3, the stock price evolves according to a lognormal process with a mean of $\mu = 10\%$ and a volatility of $\sigma = 0.3$ per year. The employer's objective is to maximize her expected utility after 5 years. Assume the employee exhibits preferences described by the utility function $U[W] = W^{\gamma}$ where $\gamma = \frac{1}{4}$. For simplicity, the employee has no wealth other than the option and may invest the proceeds from exercising the option in a riskless asset that offers the same expected return as the stock.

With these parameters, the employee is indifferent, at the date of grant, between the option and a sure payment today that gives the same utility. The sure payment today that makes the employee indifferent is \$36,960. If instead of an option that vests after 2 years, the employee receives a European option, she foregoes the opportunity to exercise early. Imposing this restriction, the corresponding sure payment today is \$30,881. Thus, the value the employee places on the American option is about 20% more than the value she places on the European option.

A risk-averse employee chooses an exercise policy that maximizes her expected utility. This policy does not, in general, coincide with the policy that maximizes the expected value of the option. Therefore, the expected cost to the employer of granting the ESO, given the employee's optimal exercise policy is less than the expected cost of an option, given an exercise policy that maximizes expected value. Option pricing models for tradable options effectively assume the exercise policy maximizes expected value. Thus, the expected cost to an employer who issues an ESO is less than the naive use of options pricing models would suggest.

To determine the cost incurred by shareholders at the date of grant of an employee stock option, one ideally would like to have a competitive market for such claims in which third parties quote a price at which they will assume the obligation to honour the call option. This market, if it existed, would clear at a price that satisfies the FASB's concept of 'fair value'. The price the employer would pay to defease the obligation is the cost of the option to the employer.

For every employee exercise policy, there exists a portfolio of the firm's stock and a riskless asset, called the hedging portfolio, that exactly mimics the payoff from the employee stock option. Provided the third party carries out the trading strategy that replicates the option's payoff, the third party bears no risk. This is because closing out the riskless asset and stock positions yields an amount that, added to the exercise price, equals the funds the employee requires to purchase the underlying stock. Competition among third parties will drive the cost of defeasing the option down to the cost of the hedging portfolio at the grant date.

This cost can also be estimated recursively from the binomial tree. Continuing the example above, the cost at the date of grant to defease a European option is \$108,879. This is also the Black-Scholes value of the option. The cost to defease an American option, assuming the employee adopts the exercise strategy that maximizes her utility, is \$94,317, about 13% less than a European option. Typically, American options are less costly to the employer and more valuable to the employee than European options. Lengthening the vesting period reduces the set of circumstances under which the employee exercises the option before maturity. Thus, postponing the vesting date lowers the value of the option to the employee and increases the cost of the option to the employer, and may increase the duration of desirable incentive effects. The increased cost to the employer may be offset by this last effect.

These relationships hold more generally. Risk aversion induces early exercise when either the option is near the money, the time to maturity is very short, and substantially all the employee's wealth is in options; or the option is deep in the money and less risky investments are available. As the set of circumstances under which the employee exercises the option (i.e. the exercise region) grows larger, the cost of the option to the employer decreases. The exercise region is jointly decided by the employer, who sets the vesting schedule, and the employee, who decides whether to exercise when exercise is allowed. The cost to an employer who issues an ESO is less than standard option pricing models for traded stock options would suggest.

This section has illustrated how employee stock options may be valued taking account of risk aversion on the part of the employees. Other reasons for exercise, such as liquidity needs or employee turnover, may similarly be modelled by specifying at each node the probability of exercise attributable to these factors.

EVIDENCE ON EXERCISE DECISIONS

As the previous section illustrated, there are many reasons why exercise of ESOs may differ from the exercise of TSOs. Direct evidence on exercise behavior serves to establish the economic significance of these factors to option valuation. Huddart and Lang (1996) analyzed patterns in exercise behavior from the detailed grant and exercise records of eight corporations over a decade. Together, these corporations issued options to almost 60,000 employees during the last decade. The sample includes a range of firms – one large industrial company, one large high-technology company, two financial services companies, three small high-technology companies that undertook initial public offerings, and an employee-owned service company. All options in the sample were fixed stock options with strike prices equal to the market price on the date of the grant. These data permit the descriptions of the general nature of grant and exercise activity and the factors associated with exercise.

The companies supplying data requested anonymity. Accordingly, they are identified by a letter code only. For brevity, I sometimes focus on the results for two companies that span many interesting patterns in the data, Companies B and H. Company B issued 10-year options that vest ratably at 25% per year. Company H issued only 5-year options that vest annually in increments of 10–40% over 4 years. Option grants extended deep into these organizations. Options were granted to 24,126 employees in Company B and 13,146 in Company H at some time during the sample period.

Univariate analysis of exercise activity

Table 1 presents summary statistics on exercise activity aggregated over all employees at the eight companies in the sample. Line 1 presents the fraction of options issued to an employee in one grant that are exercised together. The median value is 0.50, which suggests that employees generally exercise options from one grant in a few large transactions. Line 2 describes the distribution of the fraction of the life elapsed at exercise. This figure is biased downward because the data include partial histories of many option grants. Line 3 corrects for this by presenting the fraction of life elapsed at exercise for options for which more than 85% of the options' history is included in the data. The median value over all employee at the eight companies is 0.82. The median value over employee at a single company range from 0.41 to 0.96. These figures indicate that much exercise takes place well before expiration of the option, and

Table 1. Exercise activity by employee

	10%	*Median*	*90%*	*Mean*
Fraction of options granted that are exercised by an employee at one time	0.25	0.50	1.00	0.61
Fraction of life elapsed at the time of exercise*	0.13	0.39	0.97	0.46
Fraction of life elapsed at the time of exercise**	0.32	0.82	0.99	0.74
Fraction of Black-Scholes value captured at time of exercise	0.47	0.76	0.92	0.72
Fraction of Barone-Adesi and Whaley value captured at time of exercise	0.44	0.80	0.99	0.75

*All observations

**Includes only options for which more than 85% of the options' life elapsed before the end period for which exercise data was provided.

Data are based on employee-by-employee exercise activity. Decile, median and mean figures are computed over all option recipients at eight companies.

moreover, that there is variation across companies in the propensity to exercise early. Line 4 presents the ratio of the proceeds from exercise (market minus strike price) to the Black-Scholes value of the option computed at the exercise date. The median value for this variable ranges from 0.55 to 0.99 over the companies in the sample. A low value suggests employees sacrifice a large portion of the option's expected value if held to expiration. Similarly, line 5 presents the ratio of the proceeds from exercise to the Barone-Adesi and Whaley (1987) value of the options computed at the exercise date. The Barone-Adesi and Whaley computation lowers the options' values to adjust for dividends, while the Black-Scholes formula does not. Thus, the ratios on line 5 are lower than those in line 4, but also suggest substantial sacrifice of value from early exercise. The value sacrificed is greatest in the large public companies. The value sacrificed in company H is negligible. This is because employees at company H tend to hold options until maturity. The value sacrificed is also low for start-up companies that issued options with very low strike prices to employees before going public. Because the strike price on these options is a small fraction of the post-IPO market price, the intrinsic value of an option any time after the IPO nearly equals the option's Black-Scholes value, so value sacrificed is low.

Exercise and vesting

Additional evidence on exercise patterns is available in Figure 4. The unit of observation in the figure is an individual employee's decision to exercise one or more options from a given grant. There are 85,853 exercise events. The frequency of these events is plotted along two axes. One axis records the time of exercise, measured from the date of grant. This axis is divided into 6 month intervals. The second axis records the percentage of options issued to an employee in one grant that are exercised together. This axis is divided into intervals that represent ranges of 5%. Consistent with Table 1, the distribution across exercise percentages suggests that employees typically exercise options in large blocks. By far the most common block sizes are 25%, 50%, 75% and 100% of options granted. Looking over the life of the option, the mode for 25% exercise occurs in the first 6 months of the second year of option life, for 50% exercise occurs in the first 6 months of the third year of option life, for 75% exercise occurs in the first 6 months of the fourth year of option life, and for 100% exercise occurs in the second half of the fifth year of option life. The peak at the beginning of the second year of option life and 25% of options granted suggests that many employees exercise the maximum permissible number of options shortly after the first vesting anniversary. The other peaks suggest some employees wait past this anniversary, but then exercise all available options soon after a subsequent vesting date. Further, the graph confirms that much exercise takes place well before expiration.

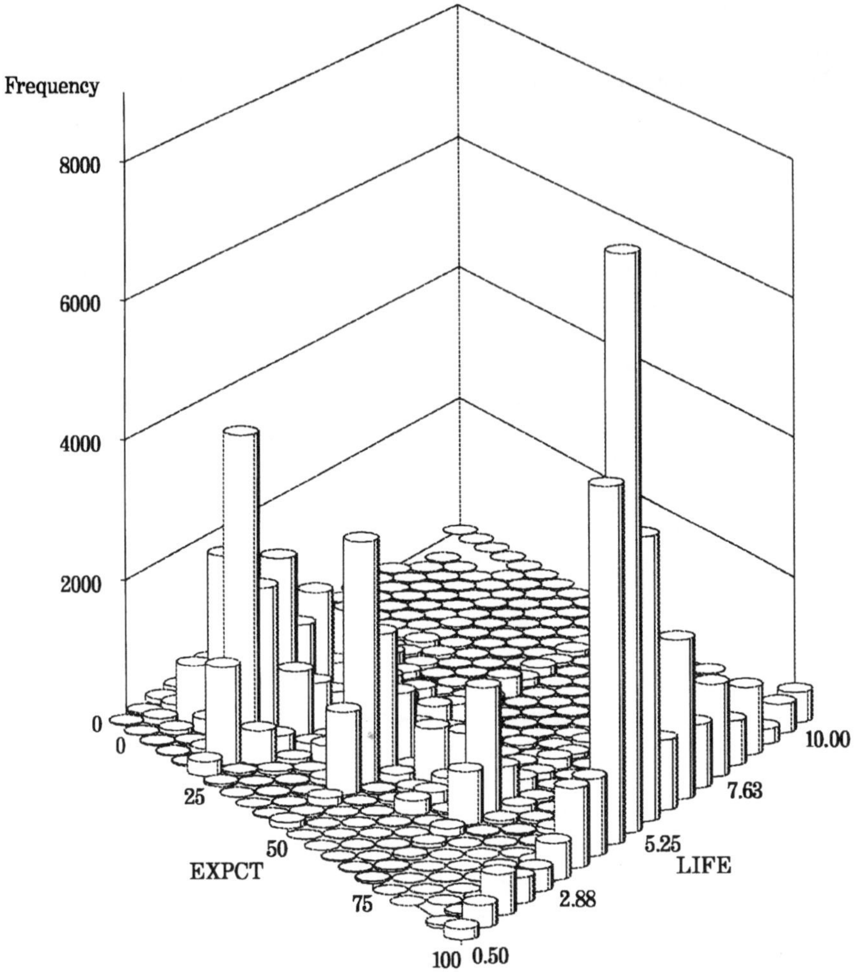

Figure 4. Frequency of exercise as a function of elapsed life and percentage of options granted. EXPCT is the percentage of options issued to an employee in one grant that are exercised together. LIFE is the elapsed life of the option in years. There are 85,853 events in which employees exercise options in our data set. The LIFE axis is divided into intervals that represent 6 month periods of time. The EXPCT axis is divided into intervals that represent ranges of 5%. In the majority of cases, employees exercise at one time exactly 25%, 50%, 75%, or 100% of the options granted to them. Exercise of 25% of the grant is clustered at the first anniversary of the grant date. Similarly, exercises of 50%, 75%, and 100% of the grant are clustered at the second, third, and fourth anniversaries of the grant. Because the common vesting schedule is 25% per year over 4 years, this pattern suggests many employees exercise options soon after they vest.

Exercise over time

Figure 5 offers a different perspective on the data prompted by the possibility that exercise activity may cluster in time since grant or calendar time. The left panels of Figure 5 present cumulative monthly exercise as a percentage of options granted for Companies B and H. In these panels, time is measured in months since the grant date. Each line corresponds to the options granted in a single calendar year.[3] Dispersion across grant-years for Company B indicates exercise patterns vary greatly. Exercise activity a given number of months after the grant date does not seem highly correlated from grant to grant.

The right-hand panels of Figure 5 contain the same cumulative exercise lines as in the left-hand panels, but the lines are aligned in calendar time instead of time since the grant date. For each company, the mid-month stock price also is plotted in the right-hand panel. If the option is out of the money in a given month, then a black dot is overlaid on the cumulative exercise curve. It is apparent from the right-hand panel for Company B that exercise clusters across grants in certain months. Further, these months appear to coincide with periods of substantial price appreciation. Thus, stock price movements appear to be important determinants of exercise for in-the-money options. This observation stands in sharp contrast to what we would expect to see for TSOs, since exercise before expiration is generally sub-optimal and not a function of either recent share price movements or time.

Company H stands in sharp contrast to Company B. Most employees at Company H wait until just before expiration to exercise the options they hold. Relative to Company B, at Company H there is high correlation across grants in cumulative exercise measured from the grant date. Also, exercise at Company H on average occurs much closer to the expiration date of the stock option than at any other company. It is apparent from the figure that Company H's stock price is much less volatile and more predictable than the stock price of any other sample company. In fact, Company H's stock price is an internally generated function of financial accounting earnings and book value.[4] Because the stock price process is more stable, the probability distribution representing the beliefs of an employee at Company H about his options' intrinsic value at any future time is probably more concentrated than the probability distributions in the minds of employees at Company B. Thus, options on the stock of Company H are much less risky. The finding that exercise occurs much later at Company H is consistent with the predicted interaction of risk aversion and volatility: employees are willing to hold less-risky options longer.

---

3 Where a company made more than one grant in a year, the amount granted is the sum of the grants made in the year, and the amount exercised in a month is the sum of the amounts exercised from each of these grants.

4 Company H makes a market in its own stock. Employees are free to sell shares acquired on exercise of options in this market. The market-maker ensures demand equals supply at the formula price through discretionary mechanisms such as stock purchases for the company ESOP.

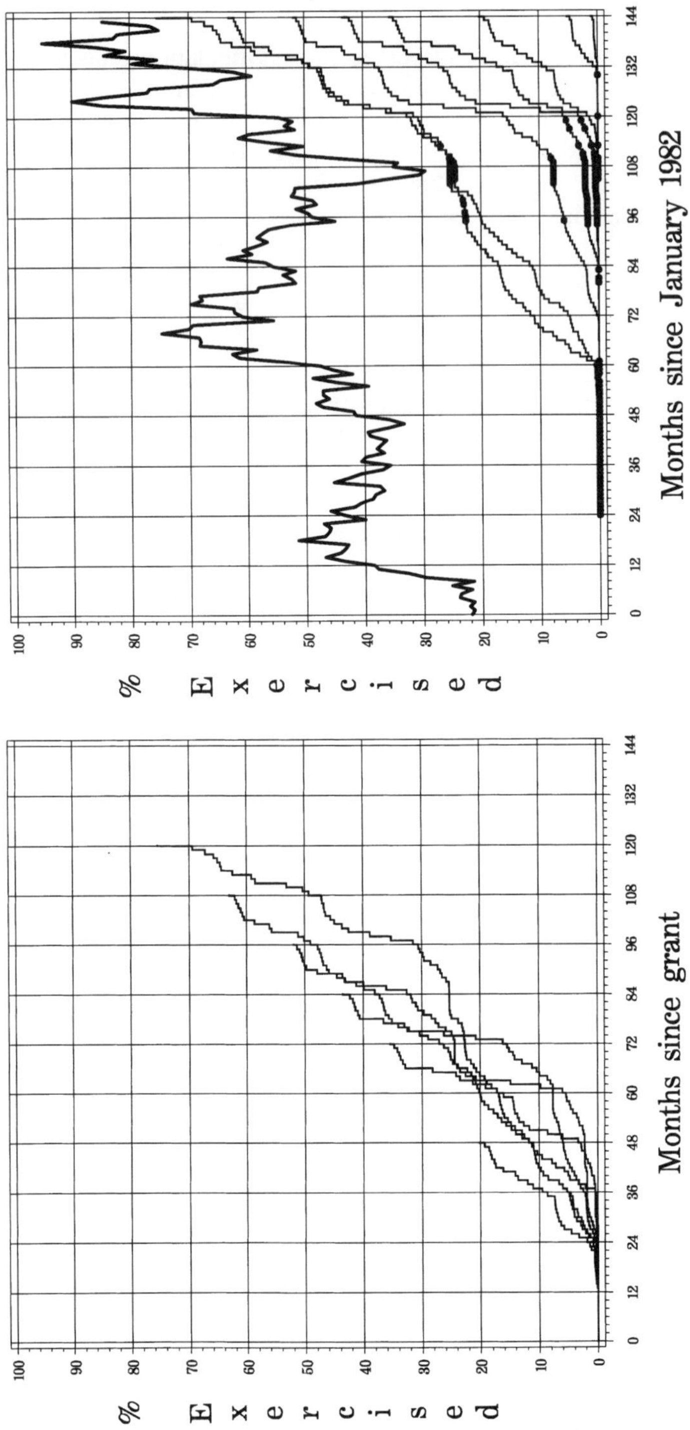
% Exercised
Months since January 1982
% Exercised
Months since grant

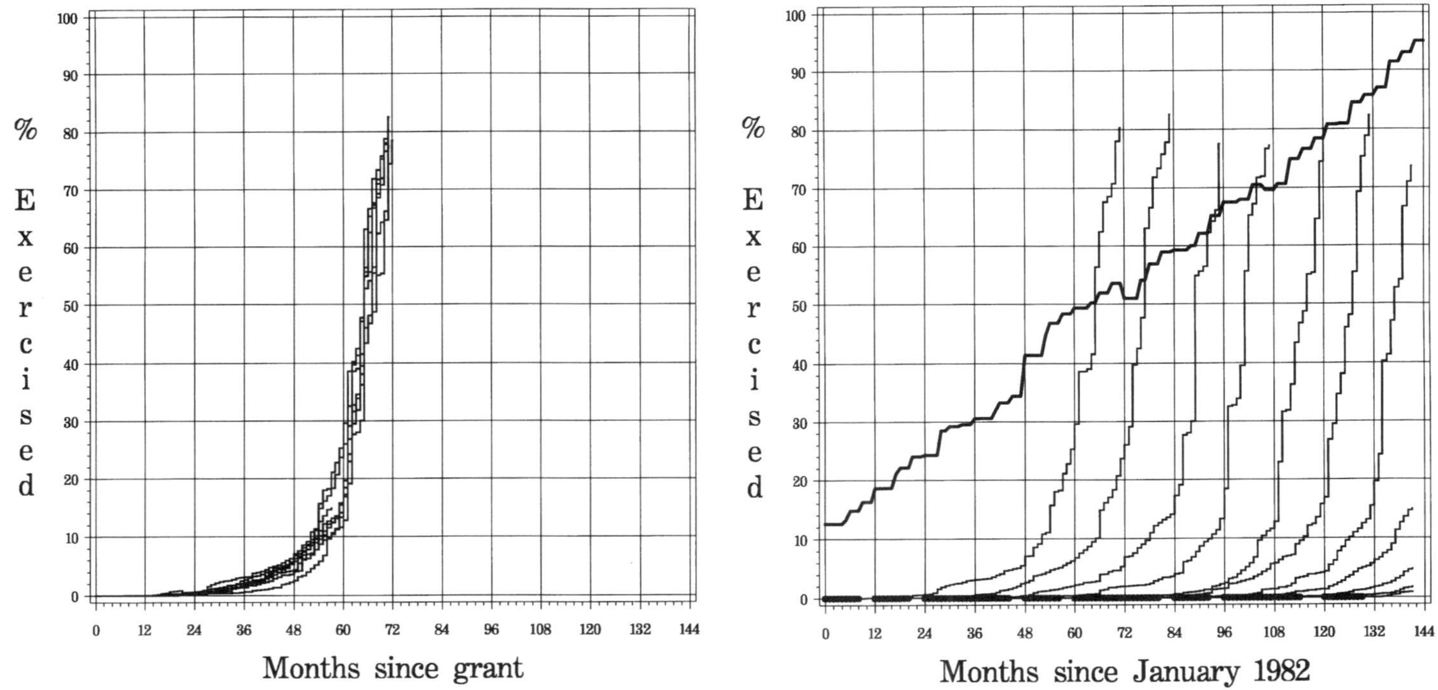

Figure 5. Cumulative exercise over time: Companies B and H. Left-hand panels: Plot of cumulative options exercised as a percentage of options granted. Time is measured from the grant date. All options granted in the same calendar year are treated as a single grant. Each line corresponds to the options granted in a single calendar year. Data were computed by cumulating the options exercised each month within grant year and dividing by the total options granted in the grant year. Right-hand panels: As in the left-hand panels, thin lines plot cumulative options exercised as a percentage of options granted, but time is measured from January 1982. Black circles overlaid on the thin lines indicate periods when the options were out of the money. The thick black line plots mid-month stock prices.

Regression analysis offers further insights. Huddart and Lang (1996) regress the fraction of options from a given grant exercised in a month on characteristics of the option in that month pooled across grants, firms, and time. The results for the seven public companies confirm returns associated with exercise.[5] Regression coefficients on contemporaneous and lagged returns strongly suggest that exercise behavior occurs in response to recent stock price movements. The relation is positive for contemporaneous and lagged returns up to 12 weeks before the exercise event. The relation is negative for the longer lagged returns, which suggests that exercise activity is path dependent: exercise occurs in periods in which the stock price is rebounding from a previous fall. The results also confirms that greater exercise is associated with higher stock price volatility.

Exercise by employee level

If factors like risk aversion and liquidity needs influence exercise behavior, exercise is likely to vary based on the personal circumstances of the employee. While data on employee-specific characteristics are unavailable, it is possible to infer something about those characteristics from an employee's level in the company. In particular, the amount and allocation across asset classes of high-level employees' wealth is likely to differ systematically from lower-level employees. The risk attitudes of employees may also differ systematically by level. Finally, the visibility of high-level employees may limit their willingness to exercise options early for fear of appearing disloyal or bearish on the company's stock.

Table 2 describes employee exercise activity in proximity to vesting dates, broken down by level of employee within the organization. Employee levels are computed according to the total number of options granted to the employee over the sample. The table shows that 64.1% of exercise events for the lowest level of employees occur in the 6 months following an option vesting date. This is nearly twice the rate for high level employees. Moreover, the fraction of exercise events that follow closely on a vesting anniversary increases monotonically across employee levels for all windows following vesting dates. The results suggest vesting schedules are less significant to the exercise decisions of high-level employees than to low-level employees.

Regression analysis by level further supports the following observations:

- On the whole, behavior is consistent across levels. Explanatory power is lower for the highest level employees, but otherwise quite comparable.
- The most pronounced differences are for historical stock price variance. The coefficient estimate on historical price variance is insignificantly negative for

[5] Company H is excluded because it is a privately-held company. Its 'stock price' for purposes of determining option value is set internally every 90 days and is therefore not comparable to the market-determined prices for the public companies.

Table 2. Exercise activity by time since last vesting date and employee rank

		Fraction of exercise activity that follows the vesting date			
Employee rank	*N*	*30 days*	*90 days*	*180 days*	*365 days*
Top 1%	2,400	0.090	0.203	0.345	0.609
Next 4%	9,398	0.118	0.258	0.414	0.726
Next 5%	9,438	0.101	0.234	0.383	0.765
Next 15%	20,553	0.113	0.265	0.436	0.804
Next 25%	21,004	0.133	0.301	0.494	0.832
Next 25%	12,431	0.162	0.332	0.541	0.862
Bottom 25%	6,734	0.196	0.390	0.641	0.883

This table displays the fraction of exercise activity that takes place within windows of 30, 90, 180, and 365 days following option's vesting dates, broken down by employee rank. Ranks are computed according to the total number of options granted to an employee within company. The 1% of employees at each company who received the most options are reported on the first line of the table, and so on. *N* is the number of exercise events over which fractions are computed.

the highest level of employees and increases monotonically across levels. The coefficient estimate is quite significant for lower levels, consistent with greater risk aversion for lower-level employees.

- Recent vesting has little effect on the exercise behavior of the highest level of employees, but has significant explanatory power for lower-level employees.
- Similarly, the coefficients on the returns variables are lowest for the high-level employees, suggesting they are less sensitive to recent stock returns.
- High-level employees are more sensitive to stock price levels than lower-level employees.

This section offers several insights. First, it appears early exercise is a pervasive phenomenon, but varies from company to company and grant to grant. Exercise is strongly positively related to volatility. Recent stock price movements and vesting dates also contribute significantly to explaining exercise. Since the results are generally similar across sample companies, employee exercise behavior seems consistent over the range of factors represented in the data. Analysis by level of employee points to differences across employees. The results are broadly consistent with predictions of the effect of risk aversion on option exercise.

For compensation design more generally, the data imply an analysis of the incentive features of options should anticipate the pervasiveness of early exercise. For example, a 10-year option may serve to align incentives for only 5 years if exercise typcially takes place then. Further, the duration of incentive effects depends on stock price performance.

Taxation

Taxation is a key factor in setting option compensation and realizing maximal value from that compensation. Exercise at opportune times may enhance the net-of-tax value of options to employees or reduce net-of-tax costs to the employer. This section summarizes employer and employee preferences for exercise before a tax rate change for all possible changes in employee and employer tax rates. It presents as a case study the exercise decisions of top executives at a major corporation before the 1993 personal tax rate increase. Then a broader investigation of tax-motivated exercise is summarized. Finally, a framework for analysing the attractiveness of exercising non-qualified options to benefit from lower capital gains tax rates is presented.

Variation in taxation across countries may be expected to result in different option granting and exercise practices. Table 3 illustrates the variety of tax treatments accorded to employee stock options across national jurisdictions. Scholes and Wolfson (1992) explain how the net-of-tax efficiency of incentive stock options compared with non-qualified options in the United States depends upon tax rates. If the corporate tax rate exceeds the personal tax rate on ordinary income then non-qualified options dominate incentive stock options. When the personal tax rate exceeds the corporate tax rate and the capital gains rate is low, then ISOs may dominate NQOs. This kind of analysis suggests that differences in tax treatment may explain variation in the use of stock options across national borders. For instance, Canada allows no deduction to employers for options exercised by employees although there is an income inclusion for the employee. Consequently, options should be used less frequently in Canada than in the USA. Mawani (1995) cites some evidence consistent with this observation.[6]

Taxation reduces proceeds from exercise. Tax planning opportunities arise if

---

[6] Financial reporting considerations also appear to influence stock option usage. Matsunaga (1995) finds use of income increasing accounting methods, such as FIFO, is associated with larger stock option grants. Moreover, tandem grants of stock appreciation rights, which would reduce reported income, and options are less likely in firms that use income increasing accounting methods. Also, earnings that are below a target level are associated with larger stock option grants. Klassen and Mawani (1998) present consistent evidence for Canadian firms.

Other evidence on stock option plan designs is more puzzling. Egginton *et al.* (1993) point out that in the UK, amounts paid to repurchase stock delivered to employees who exercise stock options are a tax deductible expense for the employer corporation, but new shares issued to employees who exercise stock options do not produce a corporate tax deduction. Furthermore, the Companies Act mandates more disclosure of option grants made under plans where exercise of options results in new stock being issued to employees than grants under plans where repurchased stock is delivered to employees. While one might expect that low disclosure and tax benefits combine to make repurchased stock plans the common choice in the UK, just the opposite is true in Egginton *et al.*'s sample.

Jennergren (1997), who considers the taxation of options in Sweden from the perspective of the tax collector, shows that alternative tax rules are not revenue neutral.

Table 3. International variation in the tax treatment accorded employee stock options

	At time of vesting	*At time of exercise*	*At time of sale*
Canada			
General rule			
Employee	None	$-(S_e - X)g$	$-(S_s - S_e)g$
Employer	None	None	None
Canadian controlled private corporation options			
Employee	None	None	$-(S_s - X)g$
Employer	None	None	None
Sweden			
General rule			
Employee	$-F_v t$	None	$-(S_s - S_e - F_v)g$
Employer	None	None	None
United Kingdom			
General rule:			
Exercise satisfied by issuance of new shares			
Employee	None	$-(S_e - X)t$	$-(S_s - S_e)g$
Employer	None	None	None
Exercise satisfied using existing shares			
Employee	None	$-(S_e - X)t$	$-(S_s - S_e)g$
Employer	None	$(S_e - X)T$	None
Approved schemes:			
Exercise satisfied by issuance of new shares			
Employee	None	None	$-(S_s - X)g$
Employer	None	None	None
Exercise satisfied using existing shares			
Employee	None	None	$-(S_s - X)g$
Employer	None	$(S_e - X)T$	None
United States			
Non-qualified stock option (NQO)			
Employee	None	$-(S_e - X)t$	$-(S_s - S_e)g$
Employer	None	$(S_e - X)T$	None
Incentive stock option (ISO)			
Employee	None	None	$-(S_s - X)g$
Employer	None	None	None

F_v, Assessed value at the time of vesting; S_e, Stock price on the day the option is exercised; S_s, Stock price on the day shares received under option are sold; X, Exercise price of the option; T, Corporate tax rate; t, Personal tax rate; g, Personal capital gains tax rate

Assumes options are granted at the money. Positive figures are reductions in taxes otherwise payable. Negative figures are incremental tax payments.

tax rates vary over time or types of income, or if rules governing the deductibility of option compensation to the employer and the timing of the employee's inclusion change. For US non-qualified options, the difference between the stock price on the exercise date and the option's strike price is taxed at ordinary rates in the year of exercise. Subsequent appreciation of stock acquired by exercise of options is taxed at capital gains rates when the stock is sold. In the last 15 years, top federal personal tax rates have ranged between 28% and 50%. Since employee stock options often have terms of 10 years, changes in tax rates potentially have an effect on the employee's exercise policy, and hence an indirect effect on the cost of the option to the employer. Non-qualified options also affect the employer's compensation cost directly since the difference between market value on the date of grant and the exercise price is a deductable expense for tax purposes.

Effects of tax on exercise – simple case

To illustrate the effects of tax on the exercise decision, consider a United States employee who holds a non-qualified option. Assume the employee seeks to maximize expected terminal portfolio value. Further, assume that the employee's exercise decision is unaffected by interim liquidity needs, the employee has no private information about stock value, and the stock pays no dividends.[7] Employee and employer marginal tax rates are about to change from t_1 and T_1 to t_2 and T_2, respectively. Let S_1 be the current stock price; X, the strike; and W_1^e, the pretax value the employee would accept today in exchange for surrendering the option. The employee favors exercise immediately before the tax rate change when the net-of-tax payment from exercise now exceeds the net-of-tax payoff from exercise after the tax rate increase, i.e.

$$(S_1 - X)(1 - t_1) - W_1^e(1 - t_2) \tag{1}$$

is positive, or

$$\frac{S_1 - X}{W_1^e} > \frac{1 - t_2}{1 - t_1} \tag{2}$$

Intuitively, if the employee exercises a deep-in-the-money short maturity option before the tax rate increase, she captures a large fraction of the option's expected total value and benefits from having this value taxed at a low rate (see Figure 6).

---

[7] Conceptually, early exercise of an employee stock option to benefit from a low tax rate resembles early exercise of a traded stock option to capture a dividend. Because traded stock options have shorter lives, they are less likely to be as far in the money as employee stock options. Thus, dividend capture is generally worthwhile only at the last dividend *ex-date* preceding option expiration, while tax factors may precipitate exercise of options that are years from expiration.

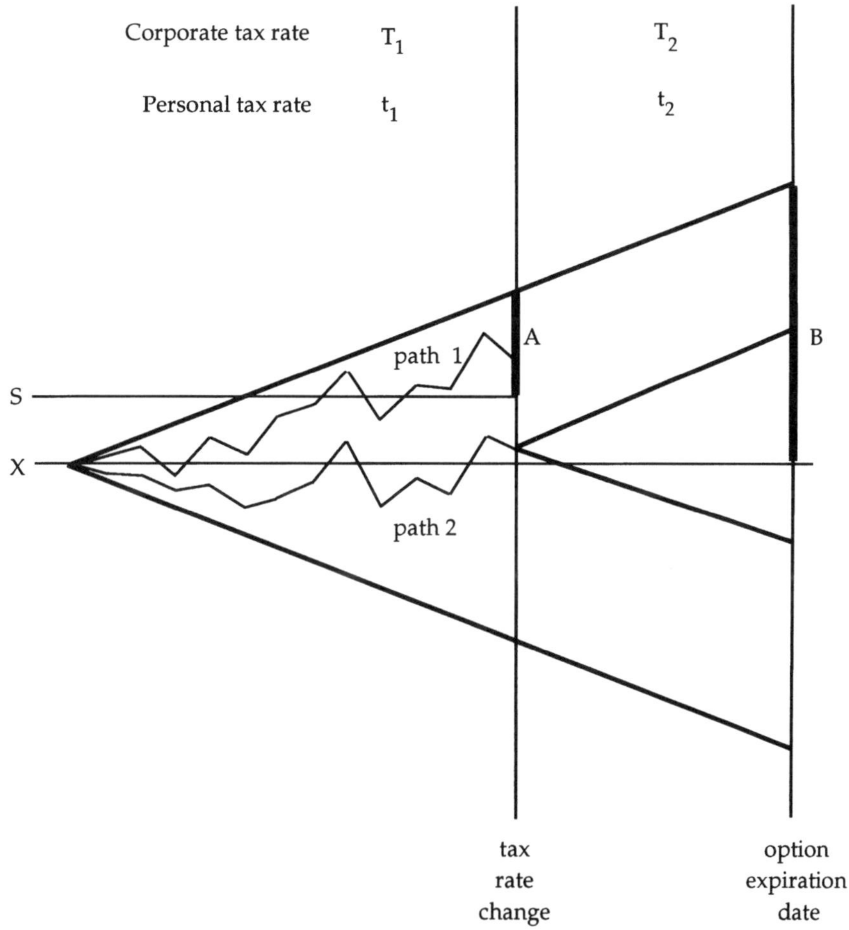

Figure 6. Relationship between stock price and exercise decisions. Consider an option on a stock that does not pay dividends. In the figure, X is the strike price and S is the least stock price at which exercise before the tax rate increase is worthwhile. The horizontal axis represents time. The vertical axis represents stock price. A risk-neutral employee who does not face liquidity constraints may choose to exercise an option just before a tax rate increase (region A) provided the stock price is high. Otherwise, the employee will exercise the option at maturity if it is in the money (region B). The exercise decision depends on the dynamics of the stock price process the options' characteristics. It is not optimal to exercise near the money options, but it may be optimal to exercise deep-in-the-money options.

Employees must also consider the likelihood that future tax rates will differ from current tax rates. If tax rates are unlikely to increase, then the attractiveness of early exercise is reduced commensurately. If tax rates were to rise only temporarily, so that the option expires after the temporary tax rate increase reverses, then there is no tax benefit to early exercise because the employee could postpone exercise until after the reversal.

Case study

Following the election of President Clinton on November 3, 1992, there was widespread expectation that personal income tax rates for high levels of income would increase in 1993. Option exercises by insiders putatively motivated by tax factors were widely reported in the business press.

There was little uncertainty whether tax rates would increase, but there was considerable uncertainty over the income level at which higher tax rates would apply and whether the increase would be effective from January 1, 1993. In fact, tax rates did rise on this date. Moreover, the tax rate rise affected more people than 1992 press reports suggested, because the 36% bracket applied to taxable income over $115,000, and the 39.6% bracket (which embodied the Clinton proposal of a 10% surtax on millionaires) applied to taxable income over $250,000 for individuals filing jointly.

The importance of tax considerations is illustrated by the actions of Michael D. Eisner and Frank Wells, respectively Chairman and late President of Disney. In the last quarter of 1992, when Disney stock was trading at $40 per share, these executives exercised 6,640,000 options expiring in 1994 with a strike of $3.59 per share. Salary and bonus levels for Eisner and Wells show they are in the top California and federal tax brackets. If Eisner and Wells believed the top federal rate would rise from 31% to 36% in 1993, a 10% federal surtax would be applied in 1993, and California state income tax would remain at 11% for 1993, then they expected to receive after tax $(1 - 11\%)(1 - 31\%) = 61.4\%$ of an incremental dollar of income reported in 1992; and, $(1 - 11\%)(1 - 36\%(1 + 10\%)) = 53.8\%$ of an incremental dollar of income reported in 1993 or later. That is, for every dollar of income triggered in 1992, 61.4¢ is left after tax, while for every dollar of income triggered in 1993 or later, only 53.8¢ (or 12% less) is left after tax. This makes the early exercise of options held by Eisner and Wells attractive from their perspective. An estimate of the tax avoided by accelerating exercise is $(61.4\% - 53.8\%) \times (\$40.00 - \$3.59) \times 6{,}640{,}000$ or $18 million. This benefit is offset by the acceleration of tax and strike price payments and by the diminished opportunity to participate in future appreciation of the stock. The net benefit is greatest when the option is deep in the money and the time to maturity is short.

Significantly, Eisner and Wells also held, but did not exercise, options expiring in 1999 with strike prices of $17.14 and $19.64.[8] Let the Black-Scholes value of the option proxy for the pretax present value of the expected payoff from the option if held to maturity. Then $(S_1 - X)/W_1^e$ is 0.9951, 0.8070, and 0.7607, for the options with strike prices of $3.59, $17.14, and $19.64,

8 See David J. Jefferson, Disney Officials Get $187 Million From Stock Sale, *Wall Street Journal* (December 2, 1992) p. A3.

respectively.[9] The option income of these executives would be taxed at an estimated rate of 38.6% in 1992 or 46.2% in 1993. Thus, $(1 - t_1)/(1 - t_2) = 0.8754$. These calculations and relationship (2) suggest that tax factors can explain the decisions by Eisner and Wells to exercise the \$3.59 options, and to not exercise the \$17.14 and \$19.64 options.

Employer preferences

From Disney's perspective in late 1992, early exercise preserves a deduction for compensation expense that might otherwise be lost because of a legislative proposal to deny a deduction for compensation about \$1 million paid to any one person. Thus, Disney would favor early exercise to assure itself of the deduction, worth about 34% of the difference between the market value of the stock and the exercise price of \$82.2 million.[10]

More generally, the employer's preference with respect to the optimal time to exercise the option do not, in general, coincide with those of the employee. The employer may find it worthwhile to induce the employee to exercise (or not exercise) before rates change. If it were up to the employer to decide when to exercise the option, he would compare the after-tax cost of compensation paid to the employee under early exercise, $(S_1 - X)(1 - T_1)$, with the expected after-tax cost of compensation to be paid to the employee when exercise is postponed until after the tax rate change, $W_1^r(1 - T_2)$, where W_1^r is the pretax present value of the expected cost of the option. Thus, the employer favors early exercise if:

$$\frac{S_1 - X}{W_1^r} < \frac{1 - T_2}{1 - T_1} \tag{3}$$

The employee and employer both favor early exercise when (2) and (3) both hold. It is also possible the employer may favor early exercise while the employee favors exercise at maturity. The employer could induce the employee to exercise early (or surrender the option if it is out of the money) by offering to pay the employee an amount, F, contingent on early exercise. For this proposal to be acceptable to the employee, F has to satisfy

$$(\max(S_1 - X, 0) + F)(1 - t_1) \geq W_1^e(1 - t_2).$$

The employer finds paying F worthwhile if

$$(\max(S_1 - X, 0) + F)(1 - T_1) < W_1^r(1 - T_2).$$

---

[9] The Black-Scholes value is estimated using a short Treasury note yield of 5.03% and estimated volatility for Disney stock of 27% per year.

[10] As enacted, §162(m) of the Internal Revenue Code does not apply to most stock option compensation.

Table 4. Effect of tax rate changes on employer and employee exercise preferences

Situation		*Preference* *Early exercise*	 *Exercise at maturity*	*Defining criteria*	*Necessary condition for gains from aligning preferences*
1	Employer	X		$\frac{S_1-X}{W_1^r} \leq \frac{1-T_2}{1-T_1}$	
	Employee	X		$\frac{1-t_2}{1-t_1} \leq \frac{S_1-X}{W_1^e}$	
2	Employer	X		$\frac{S_1-X}{W_1^r} < \frac{1-T_2}{1-T_1}$	Paying the employee F to induce early exercise is worthwhile if
	Employee		X	$\frac{S_1-X}{W_1^e} < \frac{1-t_2}{1-t_1}$	$\frac{1-t_2}{1-t_1} < \frac{1-T_2}{1_T1} \frac{W_1^r}{W_1^e}$
3	Employer		X	$\frac{1-T_2}{1-T_1} \leq \frac{S_1-X}{W_1^r}$	
	Employee		X	$\frac{S_1-X}{W_1^e e} \leq \frac{1-t_2}{1-t_1}$	
4	Employer		X	$\frac{1-T_2}{1-T_1} < \frac{S_1-X}{W_1^r}$	Paying the employee F to exchange American options for European
	Employee	X		$\frac{1-t_2}{1-t_1} < \frac{S_1-X}{W_1^e}$	options is worthwhile if $\frac{W_1^r}{W_1^e} \frac{1-T_2}{1-T_1} < \frac{1-t_2}{1-t_1}$

The employee and employer prefer the same exercise policy in Cases 1 and 3. In Cases 2 and 4, the employer and employee have opposite preferences. Depending on the values assigned to the option by the employee and employer and the tax rates, it may be worthwhile for the employer to pay the employee an amount $F = W_1^e(1 - t_2)/(1 - t_1) - \max(S_1 - X, 0)$ in exchange for a commitment to (i) exercise before the tax rate change (Case 2), or (ii) postpone exercise until after the tax rate change (Case 4).

There are two other possibilities: both the employer and employee favor exercise at maturity, and the employee favors early exercise but the employer does not. Table 4 summarizes all possibilities. In a situation that closely corresponds to situation 2 in Table 4, Matsunaga *et al.* (1992) provide anecdotal and empirical evidence on the prevalence of payments to compensate employees engaging in a disqualifying disposition of incentive stock options. The next section considers a specific instance of situation 1.

Empirical examination of the 1993 tax rate increase

Are tax considerations widely appreciated by optionees? Figure 7 summarizes Huddart's (1998) examination of the exercise behavior of a subset of more than 30,000 of the employees studied by Huddart and Lang (1996) for whom 1993 salaries were also available. Employees' option positions following the election of Clinton in 1992 were tabulated according to their intrinsic ratio, the fraction of the options' total pretax value that would be realized on exercise (i.e. $(S - X)/W_1^e$ using the notation developed above where the Barone-Adesi and Whaley, 1987, value of the option proxies for W_1^e). Options with higher intrinsic ratios are more likely to be exercised before the anticipated tax rate increase. Option positions were further subdivided by the salary level of the employee, to test the hypothesis that employees with higher salary could expect to face higher rates of tax in 1993 and therefore be more likely to exercise options late in 1992.

To control for the other factors affecting exercise, the fraction of options exercised for each salary category and intrinsic ratio level for the same periods in 1990, 1991 and 1993 were also calculated. The differences between the

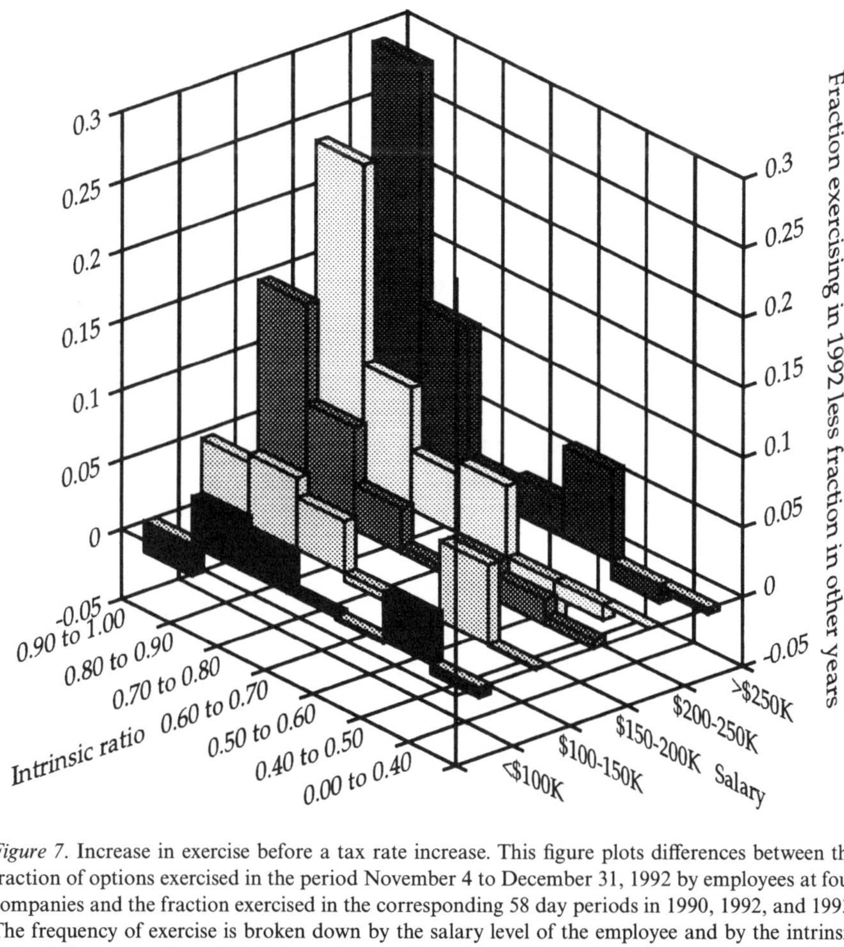

Figure 7. Increase in exercise before a tax rate increase. This figure plots differences between the fraction of options exercised in the period November 4 to December 31, 1992 by employees at four companies and the fraction exercised in the corresponding 58 day periods in 1990, 1992, and 1993. The frequency of exercise is broken down by the salary level of the employee and by the intrinsic ratio of the option $(S - X)/W$. The intrinsic ratio measures the fraction of the option's total value that would be captured on exercise. Total value is the Barone-Adesi and Whaley (1987) value of the option.

fraction exercised in 1992 and the other years are reported in Figure 7. Set against an overall likelihood of exercise of less than 3%, there is a 10-fold increase in exercise of options with high intrinsic ratios held by high salary individuals in 1992. Consistent with the tax hypothesis, the frequency of exercise attenuates as either the intrinsic ratio or the employee's salary decreases.

While this evidence suggests some employees do respond to tax factors, it also suggests that many employees who stand to benefit from early exercise to avoid higher expected tax payments do not do so. Two-thirds of the employees with highest incomes holding the options with the highest intrinsic value did not exercise. Because the trade-off is complex, it is possible that some employees were unaware of the benefits to be realized. Compensation consultants may wish to take note because similar planning opportunities arise because of the recent cut in capital gains tax, as the next section explains.

Exercise to benefit from capital gains rates

This section derives a condition on anticipated stock returns that make it worthwhile for the employee to exercise the option early so that subsequent appreciation in the stock is taxed at capital gains rather than ordinary rates.

To exercise the option and hold the stock, the employee must pay his employer the exercise price, X. The employee must also pay tax on the appreciation realized at the time of exercise of $(S_1 - X)t$. Thus, the amount of employee must borrow until the stock is sold is $X + (S_1 - X)t$. Assume the employee plans to hold the stock long enough to qualify for capital gains treatment. Further assume the option is sufficiently far in the money that the probability the option will be out of the money over the remainder of its life is remote enough to be ignored. Let the price of the stock at the time the employee would exercise the option and sell the stock absent tax considerations be $\tilde{S}_2$. Let r be the optionee's net-of-tax cost of borrowing. Exercising the option at time 1 so that future appreciation is taxed at capital gains rates is preferred if

$$\tilde{S}_2 - (\tilde{S}_2 - S_1)g - [X + (S_1 - X)t](1 + r) > (\tilde{S}_2 - X)(1 - t).$$

The left-hand side of this expression represents the cash flows at time 2 from the employee's perspective if the option is exercised at time 1 and the stock acquired on exercise is held until time 2. There are no cash flows at time 1. At time 2, the employee receives $\tilde{S}_2$ on sale of the stock. The employee pays tax on appreciation of the stock from time 1 to time 2 at rate g. The capital gains tax due on the sale is $(\tilde{S}_2 - S_1)g$. The employee must also repay the funds borrowed (plus interest) at time 1 to fund payment of the strike and withholding taxes $[X + (S_1 - X)t]\ (1 + r)$. For early exercise to be attractive, this amount must exceed the cash flow at time 2 assuming the option is held until that time. The proceeds from holding the option until time 2 are represented on the right-hand side of the inequality. Collecting terms reduces this expression to

$$(\tilde{S}_2 - S_1)(t - g) > [X + (S_1 - X)t]r.$$

The left-hand side represents the benefit from having the appreciation of stock from time 1 to time 2 taxed at capital gains rather than ordinary rates. The right-hand side of the expression represents the cost of borrowing the strike price and withholding tax until time 2. Dividing through by S_1, and collecting terms gives

$$\frac{\tilde{R}}{r} > \frac{t + \frac{X}{S_1}(1 - t)}{t - g} \tag{4}$$

where $\tilde{R} = (\tilde{S}_2 - S_1)/S_1$ is the pretax return on the stock from time 1 to time 2. This expression offers some additional intuitions. Holding other factors constant, the deeper the stock is in the money at time 1, the more attractive is early exercise. This is so because the right-hand side of (4) decreases in S_1.

This suggests a simple bound on the anticipated appreciation in the stock from time 1 to time 2 that is necessary for early exercise to be worthwhile when tax rates are constant over time. As S_1 increases, the right-hand side of (4) tends to $t/(t - g)$. If the anticipated appreciation in the stock, relative to the cost of borrowing, does not exceed this ratio, then early exercise to benefit from taxation of future appreciation at the capital gains rate is not worthwhile. This bound holds for any current stock price and strike. If capital gains are not subject to tax and the strike price is negligible, then the bound is unity. This means the anticipated pretax return on the stock must exceed the net-of-tax cost of borrowing for early exercise to be worthwhile. However, if capital gains tax is substantial, then the hurdle may be high. For instance, if t is 40% and g is 20%, then the anticipated pretax return on the stock must be at least twice the net-of-tax cost of borrowing for early exercise to be worthwhile when the strike price is negligible compared with the current market price.[11] The multiple must be higher when the strike price is substantial. For instance, if the strike price is one-third of the current market price and the pretax return on the stock is three times the net-of-tax cost of borrowing, early exercise is worthwhile.

CONCLUSION

Stock options are an increasingly common component of compensation at all levels in many organizations. An intriguing feature of most option grants is that employees may choose to exercise their options over a window that spans several years. The paper examines the causes and consequences of employee exercise decisions in three parts. First, the binomial model of stock price movements is used to explore how employee risk aversion influences option exercise and consequently affects option valuation. Next, the exercise activity

[11] This is often the case for employees holding options granted before, and expiring after, their employer's initial public offering.

of employees at eight corporations is described and related to the theoretical analysis. Finally, the impact of taxation on stock options is analyzed and compared to sample evidence. These three explorations highlight the richness and complexity of option compensation.

References

Barone-Adesi, G. and R.E. Whaley (1987). Efficient analytic approximation of American option values. *Journal of Finance*, **42**, 301–320.

Carpenter, J.N. (1998). The exercise and valuation of executive stock options. *Journal of Financial Economics*, **48**, 127–158.

Cox, J.C., S.R. Ross, and M. Rubinstein (1979). Option pricing: A simplified approach. *Journal of Financial Economics*, **7**, 229–263.

Cuny, C.J. and P. Jorion (1995). Valuing executive stock options with a departure decision. *Journal of Accounting and Economics*, **20**, 20.

Egginton, D., J. Forker and P. Grout (1993). Executive and employee share options: taxation, dilution and disclosure. *Accounting and Business Research*, **23**, 363–372.

Huddart, S. (1994). Employee stock options. *Journal of Accounting and Economics*, **18**, 207–231

Huddart, S. (1998). Tax planning and the exercise of employee stock options. *Contemporary Accounting Research*, **15**, in press.

Huddart, S. and M. Lang (1996). Employee stock options exercises: an empirical analysis. *Journal of Accounting and Economics*, **21**, 5–43.

Jennergren, L.P. (1997). *On the Valuation of a Change in Tax Systems for Employee Stock Options.* Working Paper, Stockholm School of Economics.

Klassen, K. and A. Mawani (1998). *The Impact of Financial and Tax Reporting Incentives on Option Grants to Canadian CEOs.* Working Paper, University of Waterloo.

Matsunaga, S.R. (1995). The effects of financial reporting costs on the use of employee stock options. *Accounting Review*, **70**, 1–16.

Matsunaga, S., T. Shevlin and D. Shores (1992). Disqualifying dispositions of incentive stock options: tax benefits *vs.* financial reporting costs. *Journal of Accounting Research*, **30**(supplement), 37–68.

Mawani, A. (1995). *Cancellation of Executive Stock Options: Tax and Accounting Income Considerations.* Unpublished PhD dissertation, University of Waterloo.

Scholes, M.S. and M.A. Wolfson (1992). *Taxes and Business Strategy: A Planning Approach.* Englewood Cliffs, NJ, Prentice-Hall.

STEVE MATSUNAGA
University of Oregon

9. Discussant comments

In the past several years the topic of employee stock options has generated a substantial amount of research. In the appendix, I list a dozen recent papers from top finance and accounting journals that investigate some aspect of employee stock options. This list is not exhaustive, nor does it include a number of general compensation papers that have explored different aspects of compensation, including employee stock options. Yet, as you can see, the papers have addressed a wide variety of issues.

I believe that the major reason employee stock options have drawn such interest is that researchers have had an extremely difficult time in measuring the costs and benefits of using stock options. Despite our efforts, to a large extent both the cost (value) of employee stock options and their related benefits (incentives) remain a mystery. This is due, in part, to the multitude of factors that impact those costs and benefits, including financial reporting and tax implications. Given the difficulties in identifying and measuring these benefits, it is not surprising that some individuals observe executives reaping multi-million dollar payoffs and conclude that options are simply a means by which wealthy individuals can extract additional wealth from society. These beliefs, which are reflected in press reports in the USA and abroad, serve to enhance interest in employee stock options and spur researchers to generate more insights and empirical evidence.

The central question I am here to address is how the papers from the executive stock option section of this conference fit into this mix of research. In my opinion, both seek to provide information on the costs and benefits of employee stock options, though from distinctly different approaches. In so doing, they provide examples of both the promise and the frustrations of research in this area.

Brian Main describes how the public uproar against excessive executive compensation in Britain has led some firms to switch from stock options to other forms of long-term compensation. To the extent to which this applies, political ramifications represent yet another cost to using options that must be addressed by researchers. At the same time, the reaction by some firms (and not others) provides an opportunity to study the economic costs and benefits of

J. Carpenter and D. Yermack (eds.), Executive Compensation and Shareholder Value, 143–146.

stock options. By identifying the firms that chose to switch, and assuming that the decision reflects the net benefits of using options, we could identify the factors that affect the net benefit. Unfortunately, such a test would require a substantial amount of data which would be costly, if not impossible, to collect.

Main then examines claims from the popular press that stock options are a 'give-away' to management whereby managers are insulated from downside risk. Not surprisingly, Main shows that the use of employee stock options serves to link managerial wealth with shareholder returns. However, the use of a simulated grant pattern, as opposed to actual option grants, limits the conclusions we may draw from the study. Because the granting of options could alter the distribution of future stock price changes, deviations from the stereotype grant pattern could also change the market returns, and hence the link between managerial and shareholder wealth.

In the absence of detailed data, Main uses the four times emoluments rule to derive a hypothetical granting pattern. This rule is intriguing, in and of itself, and it is unfortunate that sufficient data are not available to examine the extent to which firms follow that rule. It would also be interesting to see whether the rule has an economic basis. Rather than being an illogical administrative restriction, the rule could represent a heuristic that approximates an optimal granting pattern.

In summary, Main's paper provides interesting institutional background on stock options in Britain and raises a number of issues. The impact of popular sentiment against executive compensation and institutional guidelines, such as the four times emoluments rule, could provide tremendous opportunities for researchers to identify and measure the costs and benefits of options. However, a thorough study would require data that is either expensive to collect or completely unavailable.

The Huddart paper provides further examples of both the promise and frustration of research in this area. The issue of early exercise of employee stock options is one of the central issues in determining both the *ex-ante* value of options granted (cost to the firm) and the incentives generated by those options (benefit to the firm). Huddart's paper includes excerpts from the Huddart (1994) and Huddart and Lang (1996) papers as well as a description of how changes in tax rates could affect the exercise decision.

In his 1994 paper, Huddart provides numerical examples that show how the option holder's exercise strategy can have a significant effect on the *ex-ante* value of employee stock options. He demonstrates that altering the employee's exercise strategy, the risk of the option and the risk preferences of the individual can affect the cost to the firm of granting an option. However, care must be taken when using the option values generated in the examples. Because the model depends upon the manager's unobservable utility function and contains restrictions on the manager's ability to manage risk, the model cannot be generally used to determine option values. Therefore, the option values derived in the example depend upon the assumed utility functions and risk aversion levels.

The Huddart and Lang (1996) paper presents empirical evidence on actual employee exercise patterns. Unlike Main, Huddart and Lang were able to obtain extremely detailed information on the exercise patterns of employees for eight firms. In addition to providing interesting descriptive information on how exercise patterns differ across employee levels, they provide evidence of a relation between share price patterns and exercise decisions. In particular, they show that exercise tends to occur after share price increases that follow share price decreases. The relation between risk and exercise patterns documented by Huddart and Lang (1996) is one of the key aspects of that paper. Their evidence indicates that lower level employees tend to be more sensitive to risk than higher level employees. This result is consistent with the evidence in Hemmer *et al.* (1996) that top level managers might have their risk hedged by the firm and the evidence in a recent working paper by Ofek and Yermack that executives sell shares in their portfolio to reduce their exposure to risk. The results in these papers also have implications for the use of reload provisions that can be used to encourage early exercise of stock options.

In short, these papers address some of the central issues associated with options. Whether we are examining the effects of public pressure on compensation contracts or the factors that affect the tendency to exercise options early, we are learning more about executive compensation contracts and can better assess the costs and benefits of one of the most controversial issues we have seen in accounting and finance. As research progresses in this area we continue to discover new factors and implications associated with the use of employee stock options. In so doing, we learn more about the nature of the contracting process, the effects of incentives on managerial decisions, and the economic effects of external administrative rules and regulations. Given the changes in disclosure requirements, and continuing innovations on the structure of executive stock options, I expect this area to be a fertile ground for research in years to come.

Appendix

List of recent research papers on employee stock options

Aboody, D. (1996). Market valuation of employee stock options. *Journal of Accounting and Economics*, **22**, 357–391.

Carpenter, J. The exercise and valuation of executive stock options. *Journal of Financial Economics*, **48**, 127–158

Cuny, C.J. and P. Jorion (1995). Valuing executive stock options with endogenous departure. *Journal of Accounting and Economics*, **20**, 193–205.

Dechow, P., A. Hutton and R. Sloan (1996). Economic consequences of accounting for stock-based compensation. *Journal of Accounting Research*, **34**(supplement), 1–20.

Hemmer, T., S.R. Matsunaga and T. Shevlin (1996). The influence of risk diversification on the early exercise of employee stock options by executive officers. *Journal of Accounting and Economics*, **21**, 45–68.

Hemmer, T., S.R. Matsunaga and T. Shevlin. Optimal exercise and the cost of granting employee stock options with a reload provision. *Journal of Accounting Research*. forthcoming.

Huddart, S. (1994). Employee stock options. *Journal of Accounting and Economics*, **17**, 207–231.
Huddart, S. and M. Lang (1996). Employee stock option exercises: an empirical analysis. *Journal of Accounting and Economics*, **21**, 5–43.
Matsunaga, S.R. (1995). The effects of financial reporting costs on the use of employee stock options. *The Accounting Review*, **70**, 1–26.
Matsunaga, S.R., T. Shevlin and D. Shores (1992). Disqualifying dispositions of incentive stock options: tax benefits versus financial reporting costs. *Journal of Accounting Research* **30**(supplement), 37–68.
Yermack, D. (1995). Do corporations award CEO stock options effectively?, *Journal of Financial Economics*, **39**, 237–269.
Yermack, D. (1997). Good timing: CEO stock option awards and company news announcements, *Journal of Finance*, **52**, 449–476.

JOHN SAMUELS
University of Birmingham, England

Discussant comments

The paper by Steven Huddart is an excellent synthesis of the research into the timing of the exercise of options. Two worrying features of the conclusions are that 'early exercise is a pervasive phenomenon' and that 'exercise is strongly positively related to volatility'. The first of these findings does not fit well with one of the key justifications for executive option schemes, namely goal congruence; particularly if the goals of the corporation are other than short term.

The finding with regard to volatility can be linked to the well established fact that the potential gains from holdings options in any security increases with the volatility in price of that security. Research undertaken in the UK has shown that it is not just executives of successful companies that gain from share option schemes; the directors of a poor performing company can also obtain high rewards (Samuels and Lymer, 1996). One situation where this can occur is when options are granted at exercise prices following a period of relatively low performance and subsequently a takeover bid is received for the company (possibly more than one bid). The acquirer forces up the market price. The option is granted to the executive at the depressed price and exercised at the takeover price (Williams, 1994).

There is always a danger than the benefits to executives of a volatile share price could influence decisions made in the company, on such matters, as investment decisions and methods of obtaining finance.

One aspect of executive share options that makes them attractive in the UK is 'lapsing'. This is similar to 'repricing' in the USA. As Brian Main explains in his paper there are guidelines in the UK as to the maximum amount of executive stock options that should be held by an executive. The maximum is based on the relationship between the executives level of emoluments and the number of options held times their exercise price. What happens if the options become out of the money? If an executive holds onto these options he or she (because of the maximum value guidelines) is restricting the opportunity for the company to issue more options to them at what would be a lower exercise price.

One tactic is to surrender the old high exercise price options (to allow them

J. Carpenter and D. Yermack (eds.), Executive Compensation and Shareholder Value, 147–148.

to lapse) and to receive in exchange a larger number of lower exercise price options (the options having effectively been repriced). The executive will have to wait for another qualifying period to elapse before being allowed to exercise the options, but the potential gain is much higher. This tactic again benefits from a volatile share price.

As Brian Main points out, the use of option based and share based incentive schemes for executives is a controversial issue in the UK. One reason for this is because at the time state-owned companies are privatized, the shares are usually underpriced when sold to the public. This is because governments undertaking the privatization process wish it to be seen as a success, and one way to demonstrate this is for the issue to be many times oversubscribed. One group who benefit from this underpricing of privatization issues are the executives who receive share options that can be exercised at the issue price. When, following privatization, the market price rises to near its true (intrinsic) price, the executives receive very large rewards – not being the result of their own efforts but of a political process. With privatization taking place in many countries in the world, the same situation is presumably occurring as that which occurred in the UK.

Finally one issue should perhaps be raised at a conference on executive compensation that has not so far been mentioned, namely executives' pensions. This is clearly part of the executive compensation package but because of the way academics divide up issues into different subject areas pensions are usually considered separately from options. In the UK there has in the 1990s been less transparency on the costs and benefits of executives' pensions than on executives' option schemes, Because of this lack of awareness this form of reward has received less public comment than option schemes. There is evidence however that the benefits to directors in some years from increases in accrued pensions can be very high, equal to or in excess of those from option schemes (Samuels and Piper, 1998). These high benefits follow from large increases in an executives' basic salary, from payments by the company of executives' tax liabilities, and from generous credits for years of service.

References

Samuels, J.M. and A. Lymer (1996). Financial reporting of directors share options. *British Accounting Review*, **28**, 249–266.

Samuels, J.M. and A. Piper (1998). Directors financial rewards in the water industry. *Corporate Governance*, **6(3)**, 174–187.

Williams, A.P. (1994). *Just Reward? The Truth About Top Executive Pay.* Kogan Page, London.

List of contributors

Jennifer N. Carpenter

Jennifer N. Carpenter is an assistant professor of Finance at the New York University Stern School of Business. She received a BS in Economics from the University of Pennsylvania in 1987, an MA in Mathematics in 1993, and a PhD in Finance in 1995. She also worked for two years in the Fixed Income Division of Goldman Sachs. Professor Carpenter's research interests include executive stock options, option-like compensation for portfolio managers, and derivatives. She teaches a course in fixed income securities.

Martin J. Conyon

Martin J. Conyon received his PhD in Economics from the University of Warwick, UK. He was then a lecturer at the Queen's College, University of Oxford. He is currently a Reader in the Business School at Warwick University. His research interests are on performance determination and corporate governance. He has advised policy makers and companies on compensation, governance and performance matters.

Brian J. Hall

Brian J. Hall is an Associate Professor of Business Administration at the Harvard Business School. Previously, he was an Assistant Professor of Economics in the Harvard Economics Department. Professor Hall received his BA, MA and PhD in Economics from Harvard and also holds an M.Phil in Economics from Cambridge University. Professor Hall teaches and researches in the area of corporate finance, compensation and incentives. He is the recipient of several teaching prizes, including the 1997 Phi Beta Kappa Prize for excellence in teaching.

J. Carpenter and D. Yermack (eds.), Executive Compensation and Shareholder Value, 149–154.

Kevin F. Hallock

Kevin F. Hallock is an Assistant Professor of Economics and of Labor and Industrial Relations at the University of Illinois at Urbana-Champaign. His research is focused on applied labour economics and corporate finance. In particular, he is currently studying executive compensation, salesforce compensation, and incentives. He has published in the American Economic Review, the Journal of Financial and Qualitiative Analysis and co-edited (with Orley Ashenfelter) four volumes on Labor Economics. Hallock's research has been supported from various sources, including the American Compensation Association and the Intel Corporation. He serves as a consultant on executive compensation including recently for the United States Department of Labor on the link between executive pay, layoffs, and firm performance. Hallock received a bachelors degree in economics from the University of Massachusetts at Amherst in 1991 and a PhD in Economics from Princeton University in 1995.

Steven J. Huddart

Steven J. Huddart teaches managerial accounting and tax planning. He has published research on the effect of ownership structure on corporate value, and the cost of employee stock options. He is currently researching the role of stock options in compensation, tax planning, and financial reporting; the effects of taxation, reputation, and performance fees on portfolio choice by investment advisers; and the consequences of differing national accounting standards on the allocation of trading volume across stock exchanges. He has also published cases on indirect cost allocation and the taxation of a corporate acquisition. He is a member of the Institute of Chartered Accountants of Ontario. Currently on the faculty at Duke University, he has also taught at Stanford and Michigan.

Steven N. Kaplan

Steven N. Kaplan is the Leon Carroll Marshall Professor of Finance at the Graduate School of Business (GSB) of the University of Chicago. He has been a member of the faculty since 1988. Professor Kaplan earned his PhD in Business Economics from Harvard University. He received his A.B., *summa cum laude*, in Applied Mathematics and Economics from Harvard College. Prior to completing his PhD studies, Professor Kaplan held positions with Kidder, Peabody & Co. and Booz, Allen & Hamilton. Professor Kaplan's research, teaching and consulting focus on issues in corporate governance, corporate restructuring, entrepreneurial finance, private equity, and corporate finance. He has published papers in *The Journal of Finance, The Journal of Financial Economics, The Journal of Political Economy, The Quarterly Journal of Economics, The Journal of Applied Corporate Finance*, and *The Journal of Law, Economics and Organizations.* Professor Kaplan serves on the editorial board of *The Journal of Finance, The Journal of Financial Economics, The Journal of*

Financial and Quantitative Analysis, and *European Financial Management*. He is also a Research Associate at the National Bureau of Economic Research. Professor Kaplan testified about his research at the US Senate Finance Committee Hearings on Leveraged Buyouts. Professor Kaplan teaches advanced MBA and executive courses in corporate financial management and in entrepreneurial finance and private equity. Professor Kaplan was named one of the top twelve business school teachers in the United States in *Business Week's* 1994 survey of MBA programs. He was named one of the top four teachers of entrepreneurship in the United States in *Business Week's* 1996 survey. Professor Kaplan was also the top-rated teacher at the GSB in *Business Week's* 1992, 1994, and 1996 surveys. Outside of the GSB, Professor Kaplan co-edits Finance Case and Teaching Abstracts (of the Financial Economics Network), an Internet-based distributor of teaching materials to other academics. He also has conducted seminars in finance for corporate financial managers, bankers, lawyers, and judges. Professor Kaplan serves on the GSB Policy Committee (faculty committee to advise the Dean on GSB policy issues), the board of directors of the American Finance Association, and the board of directors of Bank of America Illinois' Community Development Corporation.

Brian G.M. Main

Brian G.M. Main studied physics at the University of St. Andrews on a United Kingdom Atomic Energy Authority industrial scholarship which mixed work experience and study. In 1970 he graduated with an MBA from the University of California, Berkeley, and worked for two years as a production planning manager for Eli Lilly at one of their UK production facilities. In 1972 he returned to Berkeley to study for a PhD in Economics. His doctoral supervisor was George Akerlof. In 1976 Brian became lecturer in Economics at the University of Edinburgh, leaving in 1987 to become Chair of Economics at the University of St. Andrews. He returned to a Chair in Economics at Edinburgh in 1991. In 1995 he also became an Executive Director of The David Hume Institute, a law and economics oriented think tank.

His primary area of research has been labor economics, and he has published fairly widely (AER, ASQ, EJ, JHR, JoLE, OEP, REStat, and so on). In recent years his work has focused on aspects of top executive pay and corporate governance.

Steve Matsunaga

Steve Matsunaga came to the University of Oregon after receiving his PhD in accounting from the University of Washington in 1992. Steve also has a BA in accounting from San Francisco State University and an MBA from The College of William and Mary. His papers on stock options have been published in The Accounting Review, Journal of Accounting Research and Journal of Accounting and Economics. Steve also currently serves on the editorial board of two American Accounting Association publications, The Accounting Review and Accounting Horizons. He received the 1994 Competitive Manuscript Award from the American Accounting Association for his paper, 'The Effects of Financial Reporting Costs on the Use of Employee Stock Options', and the 1995 Outstanding Manuscript Award from the American Taxation Association for his paper co-authored with Terry Shevlin and D. Shores, 'Disqualifying Dispositions of Incentive Stock Options: Tax Benefits Versus Financial Reporting Costs'.

Todd T. Milbourn

Todd Milbourn joined the London Business School as an Assistant Professor of Finance in August of 1996. He received his PhD in Finance at Indiana University and was a visiting Professor of Finance at Indiana University's School of Business for one year. He holds a Bachelor of Arts degree from Augustana College, Illinois, where he majored in economics, mathematics and finance.

Todd's research and teaching interests are generally centred around corporate finance topics, but he focuses his research primarily on issues of managerial compensation design, economics of asymmetric information, and capital allocation schemes. Examples of some of his current research include theoretical and empirical examinations of managerial compensation, the impact of a firm's architecture on financial decisionmaking, and capital budgeting. Todd has published articles in *Financial Analysts Journal*, *Journal of Applied Corporate Finance*, and *The Handbook of Equity Derivatives* and has one currently forthcoming in *Sloan Management Review*. He is a member of the American Finance Association, the Financial Management Association and the American Economic Association.

At the London Business School, Todd teaches in the Corporate Finance Evening Programme and in a Finance elective entitled 'Mergers, Management Buyouts and Other Corporate Reorganization'. He also teaches in several executive education programmes and acts as a consultant to several companies.

Arthur H. Rosenbloom

Arthur H. Rosenbloom is Special Partner and former Chairman of the Board of Patricof & Co. Capital Corp., a New York City based firm specializing in mergers and acquisitions, private placements and valuations of going concern businesses for tax and corporate purposes. Patricof has offices in New York and Palo Alto, affiliates in London, Paris, Zurich, Madrid and Munich and is part of Apax Partners, which includes Patricof & Co. Ventures, Inc., one of the world's largest international venture capital firms. He holds a Bachelor's degree from Bucknell University, a Master's degree from Columbia University, and a law degree from the Cornell Law School.

After practicing corporate law in New York City, in 1965 he joined a toy manufacturing firm as its chief legal and financial officer and, upon the sale of the business at the end of 1967, served eight years as an investment banker in New York City. From 1976 to 1982 Mr. Rosenbloom was Senior Vice President of Standard Research Consultants. Mr. Rosenbloom joined the predecessor to Patricof in 1982.

Mr. Rosenbloom's merger and acquisition advisory and valuation work has involved him with companies as diverse as Blockbuster Video, VNU, American Express, Act III Communications, Hyatt Corp., Continental Airlines, Inc., Trans Union Corp. and Singer Corporation, and he has been active in company privatizations.

Mr. Rosenbloom's contributions on investment banking related topics have appeared in *Inc.*, *Forbes*, *Business Week*, *The Harvard Business Review*, Matthew Bender's *Corporate Counsel's Annual*, *Mergers and Acquisitions Magazine*, *D&B Reports* and the *National Law Journal*. He has been co-editor of the Matthew Bender *Federal Tax Valuation Digest* and the Prentice-Hall *Handbook of International Mergers and Acquisitions*. Mr. Rosenbloom has lectured on going concern valuations and merger and acquisition matters before the American Institute of Certified Public Accountants, the Financial Executives Institute, and forums under the auspices of the Wharton School of the University of Pennsylvania, Cornell's Johnson Graduate School of Business and Cornell Law School. He is an Adjunct Professor of Finance at the Stern Graduate School of Business at New York University and an Adjunct Professor of Law at the Benjamin N. Cardozo School of Law. Mr. Rosenbloom is a Trustee of New York's Citizen Budget Commission, an independent watchdog agency on municipal and state finance, and a member of its Restructuring 2000 Subcommittee and is an active member of the panel of arbitrators of the American Arbitration Association and the New York Stock Exchange.

Joachim Schwalbach

Joachim Schwalbach received his PhD (Dr.rer.pol.) in Economics and Business Administration from the University of Bonn, 1981, and habilitation (Dr. habil.) in Business Administration and Industrial Economics, The Koblenz School of Corporate Management, 1987. He is full Professor of Business Administration, Humboldt-University Berlin, Faculty of Economics and Management Science, Chair in Marketing and International Management. He is a member of the Editorial Board of the *International Journal of Industrial Organization* (editor), *Sage Strategy Series* (editor), *Journal of Corporate Governance* (European editor), *Journal of Economics of Business*, and *International Journal of Small Business Economics*.

David Yermack

David Yermack is an associate professor of Finance at New York University's Stern School of Business, where he teaches courses in corporate finance and restructuring. He is also an adjunct professor at the New York University School of Law. Professor Yermack's academic research interests include executive compensation, boards of directors, and related topics in the area of corporate governance.

Index

J. Carpenter and D. Yermack (eds.), Executive Compensation and Shareholder Value, 155–159.